101 Things
You Don't Want
In Your Home

101 Things You Don't Want In Your Home

Welmoed Sisson, ACI

with cartoons by the author

NINOVAN BOOKS
Frederick, MD

Published by Ninovan Books
P.O. Box 1564
Frederick, MD 21702

Copyright ©2018 Ninovan Books
All rights reserved. No part of this publication may be reproduced or transmitted in any form or by any means, including information storage and retrieval systems, without express permission in writing from Ninovan Books, except for brief quotations in a review.

The author and publisher do not assume any responsibility and disclaim any liability to any party for any claim caused by reliance on information contained in this book. Always retain a qualified local home inspector to provide a report on the condition of a property.

ISBN-13: 978-0-9997165-0-2

First Printing, August 2018

*Dedicated to
J.D. Grewell*

with thanks from a grateful young lady.

Contents

Introduction 9
1   What is a Home Inspection? 13
2   How to Use This Book 17
3   On the Property 21
4   Outside the House 33
5   Decks 41
6   Roof 47
7   Foundation 55
8   Structure and Framing 63
9   Interior Surfaces 71
10 Fireplace and Chimney 77
11 Interior Elements 87
12 Electrical System 99
13 Plumbing System 117
14 Heating, Ventilation, and Air Conditioning (HVAC) 129
15 Laundry 141
16 Kitchen 147
17 Bathroom 153
18 Garage 163
19 When to Call a Specialist 171
20 Environmental Hazards 177
21 Conclusions 189
Acknowledgements 191
Appendix 193

Introduction

Since you've picked up this book, you are either a homeowner or one of the millions of people contemplating buying a home, either soon or sometime in the future. During the process, you are going to meet someone like me: a Home Inspector.

But what is a Home Inspector? Why are you going to spend money to hire someone to just look around the house? Isn't that something you can do yourself?

Well, sure you can. What we do isn't particularly difficult. You could certainly get some books from the library on how the various parts of a house work, and use that knowledge to figure out what's going on with the parts of your house. But, as some of my favorite people have reminded me, is this really the best use of your time? You would have to spend hours and hours of reading, which would include topics you're not sure are even applicable to your house, and then try to match up your reading with what's actually in the house. You can easily waste days, and you'll still have the worry that there was something you missed.

Instead, you call someone like me. We use our training and experience to go through the house and quickly spot where the problem areas are, why you should care about these problems, and give you guidelines on what action you should take.

Doesn't that sound a lot less stressful? Yeah, and I wish we had done the same thing when we bought our first house.

In 1982, my then-boyfriend Bob and I bought our first home. It was a lovely little rambler in Bethesda, Maryland. We were young and naive and had no clue there was even a profession called Home Inspector. We could reliably identify that that box in the cellar was indeed a furnace, and gosh, those bushes out back looked pretty. But we really had no clue what we were looking at. Sure, there was a little bit of a sag in the ceiling over the dining room, but it didn't look serious, so we paid it no mind. Never thought about the roof, never thought about the crawl space. We closed the deal and moved in.

About a year later the sag started getting worse. Bob got the ladder out and went on the roof (a flat membrane-style), and noticed an area with some ponding water. He figured that was probably a bad thing, and called a roofer to come take a look. The roofer told us the roof was shot, and needed to be replaced. Once the old roof was ripped off, the contractor found that the joists over the dining room did not meet the main beam of the house, which was why the ceiling was sagging. This was a pretty serious structural issue, and added quite a bit to the reroofing cost. The whole roof also had no insulation at all, which certainly helped explain why our heating bills were so high.

If we had gotten a home inspection prior to purchasing the property, the report would likely have flagged the ceiling issue, as well as the ponding in the flat roof. The inspector would have called for a roofer to do a detailed analysis of the roofing system, with testing to determine the cause of the sagging, and that this should be done before closing. We also would have learned about the moisture issue in the crawl space that had to be fixed, and the lack of insulation in there that was the reason the bedroom above the crawl space was always freezing cold. Had we known about all these issues, we could have asked the seller to repair them prior to closing, or could have asked for price concessions. But since we didn't know, they all became ours to deal with. It was an expensive lesson.

When we looked at houses, we were making the typical mistakes of uninformed home buyers: we were concentrating so hard on the layout of the house and its cosmetic features that we didn't pay any attention to the infrastructure. And that's where the expensive things are! When multiple systems that make up a house have problems, the fixes can be very, very costly.

This book can help you avoid some of the most expensive pitfalls that we've come across during our inspections. Of course, these aren't the only problems a house can have, but they are some of the more expensive to repair, or are just downright dangerous. By being aware of these issues, you might know enough to avoid putting an offer down on a house that isn't right for you. If a prospective home makes it past this first screening, then the chances of your home inspector having to spoil your dreams will be greatly minimized[1].

That's not to say that every house with one or more of the issues in this book is going to be a money pit. We have yet to come across a house that doesn't have at least one of the problems; the most common by far can be found on page 147.

---

[1] *Plus, the inspection will go so much faster, which makes inspectors happy. Fewer defects to report means writing the report takes less time.*

1
What is a Home Inspection?

So what, exactly, is a home inspection? According to the American Society of Home Inspectors, it is

> "...an objective visual examination of the physical structure and systems of a house, from the roof to the foundation."

The key word here is "visual." We can only report on what we can see. That means if there's something going on inside the walls, we're not going to be able to see it... at least, not directly. Sometimes there are clues that point to possible issues in places we can't see. It's all part of a home inspector's training to be able to read those clues and connect the dots to provide the client the most accurate possible information.

I like to compare a home inspector's job to both a detective and a storyteller. We are there to read the clues in the house, and to put together the story of how the house works, and to do it all in a way that the client will be able to understand.

Every house is different, but inspections typically follow a routine[2]. I will start by asking my client what their expectations are about the house: move-in ready? Some renovation? Do they have a budget for repairs? Then I will do a quick walk around the outside and through the house, to see where things like the attic access and the electrical panel are, and also if there are any immediate red flags that would far exceed my clients' budget to deal with[3]. Then the real inspection starts: first comes the outside, walking all the way around at least twice. If it's safe, I'll get up on the roof for a close look (not all roofs can be walked). Then I head inside and work my way through the property, starting in the attic and working my way down to the basement. On the way I look in every room, testing outlets, fixtures and windows. I check doors to make sure they work properly. I test all the bathroom fixtures, and the installed kitchen appliances. I open the electrical panel (again, if it's safe to do so), check the heating and cooling equipment, and all the other utility connections. Throughout the process, I'm taking pictures and making notes with my inspection software, either with my phone or my tablet. Once I'm done, all the notes, findings and pictures are compiled into one document, which I review with the client while we're still on site. Once back in the office, the report is compiled and finalized, and then emailed to the client.

Sometimes we will get a really huge house to inspect (I think our record was about 12,000 square feet). In those cases, both Bob and I will show up for the inspection, and we'll "divide and conquer." He'll do the mechanicals (which tend to take longer for such big houses), while I do the kitchen(s) and bathroom(s), and we split the rest.

The typical scenario for needing a home inspection is when buying a house. No matter whether it's more than a hundred years old or brand new

---

2 *Every inspector develops and follows their own routine; there really is no "right" or "wrong" way to inspect a house, as long as all the systems, elements and components are inspected according to whatever Standards of Practice the particular inspector follows.*

3 *If I find one (or more), I will point them out to the client and ask if they want to abort the inspection. If they say yes, I will typically just charge them a trip fee. I know they'll call me for the next one.*

construction, mansion or condominium, a home inspection is something you'll need for your peace of mind. Buying a house is a huge investment! It's worth getting a qualified, independent, picky home inspector to remove your emotionally tinted glasses.

However, home sales aren't the only time an inspection makes sense. Here are some other opportunities to find out what's up with a home.

- **Home Checkup**

You've lived in your house for seven to ten years. While you've been there, the house has been changing. You probably don't see it, since you're there every day. But houses age just like people do, and a home checkup can help identify areas of deferred maintenance and safety issues.

- **Pre-Listing Inspection**

Planning on selling your house in the near future? Getting a pre-listing inspection will let you repair some of the issues and defects before a buyer's inspector can flag them. The less a buyer's inspector finds, the smoother the transaction can be for everyone involved, which can more money in your pocket.

- **Estate Planning**

Real estate is usually the single largest element of an estate, so it makes sense to know what kind of shape it's in. When's it going to need a new roof? How long will the furnace last? What kinds of maintenance can be done to ensure the property maintains its value?

- **Divorce**

A divorce is never a pleasant experience. Egos and personalities all get bruised and assaulted and every imaginable button gets pushed. What once was a safe place - one's home - can become a battlefield. People who have lived in their home for years could be unaware that there may be conditions in the home which need to be addressed. What is needed is an impartial assessment of the condition of the home so that all parties can make informed decisions as to the best way to move forward to a settlement.

2
How to Use This Book

The book is organized in to sections based on the various locations and systems in and around the home. The order pretty much follows my own "flow" through a property as I do the inspection. Every inspector has their own routine, and we use these to help us not miss areas or details.

Don't think you have to read it in any particular order; it's not a novel, and each section stands on its own, so feel free to jump around to whatever interests you... or whatever happens to be of concern. Sprinkled throughout the book will be stories illustrating the ups and downs of being a Home Inspector.

The Appendix also has resources for more in-depth information on many of the topics.

The vast majority of defects in this book can be identified without the use of any tools. I recommend using a good flashlight to help spot things. For some areas, you may need a screwdriver or ladder.

Home Inspectors carry quite a few tools, but rarely use all of them during inspections. My main tools are my eyes! Aside from that, I wear a tool belt with a screwdriver, sharp awl for probing wood for rot, a small circuit tester, instant-read thermometer, and my camera. That's it!

There are more tools in my bag, of course.

- Laser thermometer
- Thermal camera
- Gas sniffer
- Moisture meter
- Garage door tester
- Water pressure gauge

In my van I've got a 17-foot foldable ladder, a 7-foot collapsible stepladder, my crawl space gear (tyvek suit, kneepads, heavy-duty gloves, respirator), and some assorted other stuff. It's no wonder the van rattles when I'm driving.

A word of warning: You should NOT open electrical panels or climb onto roofs unless you have been trained to do so safely! I'm not advocating that you do anything foolhardy in the name of saving a few bucks on a home inspection; it's just not worth it!

Some of the items in this book may seem like trivial items. Why on earth should you be concerned if there are a few bushes touching the house?[4] One of the things a home inspector will explain to you is that there may be far-reaching implications of even small defects like this. We're trained to connect the dots between what we see and what can happen.

Here's where I have to point out that some of the things I do are dangerous (like opening electrical panels and climbing ladders). If you choose to do dangerous things, I'm not responsible if you hurt yourself by doing something you really have no business doing.

So, let's get started, shall we?

---

4   *Turn to Chapter 4 to read why.*

Notes from the Field

This is is probably the most embarassing thing I did during a home inspection.

It was a new construction final walkthrough inspection, and I was in the attic, looking at the heat pump air handler installed there. Everything looked pretty good, but I wanted to get a closer look at some of the ductwork going behind the air handler.

What I thought was plywood... wasn't.

Fortunately, I had a firm grip on the truss and was able to prevent myself falling through the ceiling. Still, most of my leg went through, and I'm pretty sure I uttered a few choice swear words as I pulled myself back up and onto firm footing.

I'm very lucky to have had that handhold, too, since the spot where I went through was right over the stairwell. If I had fallen, it would have been a 12-foot drop, followed by tumbling down another 8 feet of stairs.

As it was, I spent 20 minutes cleaning up the debris from my accident, and apologizing to the site supervisor, who was trying very hard not to burst out laughing.

Ever since this little mishap, I adhere firmly to my attic policy: "If I'm moving, I'm not inspecting. If I'm inspecting, I'm not moving." This means that any time I'm actually looking at a system or component, my feet are firmly planted in place. When I move, I focus on where my feet are, and try to keep one hand on a piece of framework... just in case.

3
On the Property

Mushy Spots

When I'm walking around a property for the first time, in addition to paying attention to the outside of the house, I'm paying attention to my feet. Specifically, are they on solid ground? Mushy spots in a yard point to poor drainage... or worse, a broken sewer pipe or faulty septic system.

Drainage is a tricky element to get right, and it's so critical to the stability of the property. If we do an inspection when there's been a two-week dry spell, it can be difficult to get an accurate feel for how the water behaves as it moves on and across the property.[5] Sometimes it's possible to

---

5   *We've actually had clients who call us the day before an inspection if there's rain forecast, asking if we're planning on rescheduling because of the weather. We always tell them the ideal time for a home inspection is during a heavy rainstorm; it lets us see how well the property drains and whether the roof leaks!*

read clues, like a pattern of flattened grasses or areas of erosion. Things like mossy areas are also signs of a yard that won't dry out.

The crucial thing when encountering mushy spots is to identify the cause. If it's just water management, it can typically be handled by a landscape contractor or drainage specialist. But if it's a broken underground pipe or a failed septic system, the repair costs can easily top $10,000, not including having to make the yard look nice again after the backhoes have been there.

Smelly Spots

The human nose is quite sensitive. Pay attention to it as you're walking around the property. Some smells are normal, such as fresh mulch and mown grass. But if you smell something unpleasant... start looking for the cause.

Natural Gas: Natural gas does not have an odor of its own. Gas companies add what's called an "odorant," usually methanethiol[6]. It has a very distinctive putrid smell designed to get your attention in a hurry. That's a very good thing! Gas leaks can lead to massive explosions, obliterating not only the house with the leak but surrounding houses as well.

You should never smell natural gas (or propane, which has a different odorant[7]) when you are walking around a property, and certainly not when you are inside. There is no such thing as a small gas leak!

WARNING: If you smell natural gas or propane as you walk into a house, LEAVE IMMEDIATELY, and close the door on your way out. Do NOT operate any light switches or do anything that might generate a spark. Get well away from the property and call 911. Gas leaks are an immediate life safety hazard!

Sewage: Raw sewage has an unmistakable odor. It's also something you should never smell, either inside or outside the house. If you do, you've got a serious problem.

Sewage smell from the yard means the waste from the house is leaking from either a broken pipe or a failed septic system. Just because the pipe

---

6   *CH4S; also known as methyl mercaptan.*
7   *Ethanethiol (C3H8), also known as ethyl mercaptan.*

Why bother with a trap at all? There was nothing under this sink to keep the sewer smells out of the bathroom.

isn't inside the house, don't assume it's not your problem. Most municipal sewer systems have the owner's responsibility start where the home's pipe enters the main. To identify where the problem is, you will need to contact a drain company to stick a camera down the pipe via the cleanout in your house to spot the location of the break. Contractors will probably end up having to dig up at least a portion of the yard to get at the pipe and repair it.

If the smell is inside the house, there are a few possible causes. The simplest one is that a trap in a little-used fixture has dried out, allowing the sewer gases to seep into the house. That's an easy fix, and can be prevented by making sure all bath fixtures get run periodically.

The next possibility is that there is no trap under one of the fixtures. Any fixture with flowing water (sink, bath, shower) should have a P-trap under it. If there's no trap, you can get sewer gases in the house.

The worst-case scenario is a sewage backup. These can happen with either municipal systems or private septic systems. With municipal systems, it's usually an issue with a clogged pipe. With septic systems, it can be a clogged pipe, or it can also be the first sign of a failed system. In the latter case, the repair costs can be extremely high.

This enormous Tulip tree came within about two inches of the side of this house. A strong wind could have caused heavy damage. Removal of the tree cost the homeowner about $4,000.

Dead or Dying Trees

Home inspectors aren't arborists, but we do pay attention to the trees planted near the house. Dead trees are pretty easy to spot in the summertime; in winter it's a bit more tricky but we do our best.

Dead or dying trees can be a threat to a property because they will do a lot of damage when they fall. If there's a dead tree that is leaning towards the house, and looks like it would fall onto it, we will recommend having the tree removed. Even if the tree isn't an imminent threat, it is more likely to drop branches that can damage the roof - not to mention the noggins of anyone who happens to be underneath them at the time.

Removal of a tree isn't always a simple matter of taking a chain saw to it. It's a job best left to professionals with the proper training and safety tools. In the case of tall trees, it may be preferable for the removal company to bring in a crane, which allows them to cut the tree down from top to bottom and stack the pieces directly onto a removal truck. This protects the surrounding landscaping and eliminates the danger of having the tree fall into the house. However, there needs to be adequate clearance for the crane to get near the tree, which might mean temporary removal of fences or other obstacles.

If the tree has a large root system, removing the tree can lead to some soil collapse once those roots have rotted. A good arborist will know how to compensate for this, typically by adding soil to the area where the tree was. While it will look like a mound for a while, eventually it will sink down until it is level with the rest of the ground.

Buried Oil Tanks

For many years, the prevailing wisdom was to bury residential oil tanks in the ground to protect them from the elements and from damage. Also, they were considered "unsightly," so people didn't want to see them, either in their yards or in their basements. In northern climates, it was common to bury tanks to protect the oil from freezing temperatures, which would cause sluggish flow. Buried tanks could also be larger, avoiding the need for frequent fills. These old tanks were generally single-walled, and, while they were sturdy, they were also prone to corrosion from being in contact with damp soil. This caused oil to seep into the soil, contaminating it and creating a severe environmental hazard.

Buried tanks are considered to be imminent environmental hazards. If one is discovered, it needs to be tested to determine whether it has started to leak. This involves probing the soil around and under the tank to collect samples to test for evidence of any oil. If the tests come back positive, the tank and surrounding soil must be excavated and disposed of. This

These two pipes sticking up out of the ground in the yard are a pretty good indicator that there may be a buried oil tank on the property.

isn't as simple as it sounds: the process needs to be performed by licensed contractors, and be well-documented (with photographs, if at all possible). The Environmental Protection Agency will levy steep fines on clandestine removal.

The environmental impact of a leaking underground tank can be enormous, and it can be difficult to accurately assess the condition of a buried tank. Removal and decontamination costs can easily escalate into the hundreds of thousands of dollars. What's more, the responsibility for remediation falls on whomever owns the property at the time the leak is discovered. So, if you buy a house with a buried tank and a year later you find out it's been leaking for years, you will be responsible for all the cleanup costs.

Even above-ground tanks are subject to heavy regulation. If a leak is discovered in any oil tank, it must be reported to the EPA within two hours.

Replacing an above-ground or indoor oil tank usually costs under $2,000. But if the tank has leaked, all of the affected surrounding soil must be removed, driving up the price. And digging up a leaking buried tank can cost $10,000 or even much more, depending upon the extent of the contamination. Keep in mind too that there is no cap on remediation costs for a leaking buried tank; this means that any removal cost, no matter how high, is the homeowner's responsibility, and insurance will normally not cover it. It's not unheard of for cleanup costs to exceed half a million dollars.

In some jurisdictions, buried tanks can be "abandoned in place," usually by pumping all the oil out, cutting an access hole in the top, scouring the inside to remove all traces of fuel, and filling the tank with inert material before covering it back up again. However, more and more jurisdictions are eliminating the option to abandon in place, and require removal of all tanks not currently in use.

It's not always easy to know whether there is a buried oil tank on a property. Many were installed prior to permit requirements, and may not appear on official property records. Sometimes you can spot the fill and vent pipes in the yard. But if a tank has been abandoned in place, fill and vent pipes are typically cut off, so there is no sign of a tank from the outside. The only clue that a house has or once had a buried oil tank is

This retaining wall is leaning significantly due to the pressure of the water and soil behind it. When it falls, it will compromise the stability of the deck. It will need to be taken down and replaced, with proper drainage behind it.

often the presence of one or two metal tubes, each about 3/8" in diameter, protruding through the foundation wall in the basement.

Failing Retaining Walls

Retaining walls are used to hold back soil when the elevation difference is too great for a simple slope. Slopes greater than 45° are prone to erosion and slipping, so walls can make the ground more level and easier to maintain. Retaining walls can also be used to add visual interest to a property, and can help create flat areas on sloped properties.

That is, of course, assuming the walls were built correctly. Retaining walls are subject to enormous pressures from the water in the soil behind them. Rainwater needs to be safely drained from behind the wall; if it isn't, the wall will eventually fail.

The dirt behind a retaining wall will rarely cause problems on its own; it's the water within the soil that causes walls to fail. A cubic foot of water can exert about 65 pounds of pressure, and retaining walls typically have hundreds of cubit feet behind them. Not to mention, if you're in an area with cold winters, the water in the soil will freeze and expand, exerting even more pressure on the wall. So how do you prevent the water from causing problems?

Retaining walls should have regularly spaced drainage holes, which will be the only visible part of the drainage system. Once the wall is built and backfilled, you won't be able to see whether the proper fill materials were used, or if there are holdbacks (anchoring elements embedded in the soil behind the wall). These two elements are crucial to the overall stability and endurance of a retaining wall, especially if it is constructed with wood landscaping timbers or railroad ties..

Failure of a retaining wall can be merely a nuisance, or it can impact the stability of the foundation; much depends upon where the wall is in relation to the house. We will sometimes recommend a consultation by a structural engineer or soil engineer to determine whether a retaining wall could harm the structure if it failed. A lot depends upon whether the wall falls within the area of bearing soil under the foundation footing. This is something only an engineer will be able to determine.

Retaining walls are also used as property separators when a neighborhood is located on a sloped terrain. In these cases, it is important to determined who actually owns the wall, and who is responsible for its maintenance and/or repair. If the walls are located directly on the property line, there may need to be a contract between the two property owners to specify how the costs for the wall's upkeep are shared. Without such an

The side yard of this house sloped down towards the foundation, plus the downspout discharged too close to the house. It's no wonder the basement was wet!

agreement, it could create a dispute between neighbors, especially if they cannot agree on how to maintain or repair the wall.

Although a leaning wall may not seem like a major fix, it actually is. You cannot simply push the wall back into place; the existing wall must be removed, the soil behind it excavated, and an entirely new wall constructed, with the proper sleepers, gravel fill, and drainage holes. If only part of the wall is affected, it may be possible to only rebuild that part, but for the best long-term solution, fixing the entire wall would be a better plan.

Poor Grading

The ideal property has the house at the center, sitting at the highest point, with the rest of the grounds sloping gently away from it. Unfortunately, these properties are rare. Builders are at the mercy of topology and geology, not to mention having to work around regulations regarding conservation areas and storm water management. They are also trying to maximize their return, which means putting as many houses in as they possibly can and dealing with the terrain as best they can.

Grading is often an afterthought for some of these properties. Homeowners tinker with additions, hardscapes, and other alterations that can cause further grading issues, preventing rain water from draining away from the foundation. Water that flows toward the foundation, or puddles near it, can penetrate the structure and cause damage to the interior.

The rule of thumb is that any water that falls on the house should be carried a minimum of six feet from where the foundation meets the grade. This prevents it from seeping into the ground and being drawn into the foundation walls. This is typically the job of the gutter and downspout system[8] (See page 43), but poor grading will make it that much harder for those gutters to do their job.

Sometimes the fix is as simple as adding downspout extensions to the gutter system. However, if the issue lies with the grading of the property itself, heavy machinery will need to be brought in to recontour the affected area to redirect the water flow. This will impact anything on the affected side(s) of the house: landscaping, decks, patios, play structures... everything will have to be removed to repair the grading.

---

8 *See pages 29 and 43 for more on the importance of good gutters.*

When looking at a property, try to imagine how people will use the areas around the house. This can help you determine whether there are grading issues that could interfere with your plans. There are often visible clues that point to grading problems: spots of erosion, areas of poor grass growth, grass flattened due to water flow, or standing water.

Poor Access

Any exterior issues will become much more expensive to remediate if there is poor access to the affected area. We have seen places where the houses had what we like to call "Grey Poupon" spacing: you could open a window and ask your neighbor to hand you their bottle of Grey Poupon. Houses are built right up to the setback lines, and sometimes bumpouts for fireplaces could even extend over those lines (although they're not supposed to). Or maybe there's a lovely fence around the back yard, with a gate that's about three feet wide. Either way, the result is that there is no space to get any vehicle wider than a bicycle past that bottleneck, limiting the access to the back yard.

These are mainly annoyance issues, but if a condition arises that requires getting heavy equipment into the back yard (like a backhoe, or crane, or even a fire/rescue unit), that limited access is going to mean costly (or life-threatening) delays. Ideally, there should be a ten-foot-wide clear path to any portion of the property.

Left, the painted-over house numbers are virtually invisible, even at close range. Below, spelling out house numbers can make it harder for first responders to find you.

In the case of houses that are close together, this might not be possible. However, access might be obtained through a neighboring property. This is something to explore with the adjoining owners; you might need to draw up a formal agreement specifying the conditions under which you could bring equipment into your yard via their property.

If the issue is a fence, consider having a section of the fence redesigned to be removable. By doing so, you won't face having to knock down the fence for access. Just be sure the sections can be removed quickly in the event of an emergency, otherwise it may end up getting knocked aside anyway. Firefighters and first responders are more interested in saving lives than saving fences.

Consider, too, the importance of good signage and good lighting. House numbers should be large and clearly visible from the street; you don't want to have emergency personnel squinting to find your house when time is of the essence. For a while, there was a trend toward writing out a house number in fancy script. Our brains aren't wired to immediately recognize written numbers greater than ten; if you've got "Seventeen Thousand Three Hundred Twenty-Five" over your door, it takes a few seconds to decipher, and if you're waiting for an ambulance, time is precious. My favorite test is "25 miles per hour, at night, in the rain." If you can't see the number under bad conditions, you should fix them. Good signage will also make it easier for visitors to find you, as well as delivery companies.

As for lighting, it is important not just for security but for safety as well. Once you've lived in a house for a while, you get to know where all the little "foot traps" are: the slight bump in the front walk, or the low edging surrounding the flower bed next to the driveway. But visitors will have a hard time avoiding those obstacles, especially if they can't see them. Exterior doors are required to have at least one light on the outside, but any areas of transition - that is, where there is entry or exit, or a change of level - should be well-lit. This includes any parking area where people get in and out of vehicles, or where equipment may be operated. It's also a good idea to have lights near exterior outlets and hose bibs to make them easier to see at night.

Inspection Tales
by Welmoed Sisson, Inspections by Bob

4
Outside the House

Plants/Trees Touching the House

We've all seen picturesque cottages covered with vines, with lush bushes hugging the walls and wisteria climbing the porch posts. Sorry to burst your bubble, but these are all bad things. Plants hold moisture and prevent the house from properly drying out, which leads to organic[9] growth.

Any time you have organic material touching the house, you've got potential for water to get in, or even insects and other vermin. This can happen to the best of houses, even in high-end properties. But the landscaper didn't keep the bushes trimmed away from the living room's bay window bump-out, allowing the rhododendron leaves to stay in contact

---

9 *Remember, I can't call it "mold" as I'm not a mold specialist! Besides, you really don't want the word showing up in your inspection report; it makes lenders nervous.*

A steady stream of ants was using the rhododendron bush touching the house as a convenient pathway, and the rotted wood allowed them access to the framing and interior.

with the house, preventing the trim from drying out, which led to rot, which gave the local ant population a convenient highway into the framing.

It doesn't take much to cause structural damage to a building; all that is needed is an entry point. And if that entry is hidden from view, you might not see the damage until it spreads to the inner walls. By that time, the repair costs have skyrocketed.

Vines growing up masonry walls can cause costly damage. Vines send out supports called holdfasts that adhere to the stone and mortar. This leads to water buildup in the wall, and when that water freezes, it can cause portions of the stone to simply pop off (called spalling). Once the stone is damaged like this, it must be replaced.

In newer construction, the problem is often that trees and shrubs are planted too close to the house from the start. It may look awkward to have a small Leyland Cyprus planted ten feet away from the corner of the house, but once that tree grows up, it can have a very large circumference that will contact the house and cause problems.

Not only that, but plants and trees get buffeted by winds, which can make them strike the house and cause mechanical damage. Trees will also drop their leaves onto the roof, where they decay and cause damage to the shingles. The best way to avoid these issues is to keep plants, bushes, and trees trimmed at least six inches from any component of the house; a foot is preferable.

Gutters Draining at the Foundation

The end-unit townhouse I was inspecting was perfect for my first-time-homebuyer clients. It appeared to be in pretty good shape for its age, but there was something not quite right in the basement. There appeared to be a return air register in the front room, but it was on an outside wall, which didn't make sense. So I aimed my flashlight through the louvers to see what was behind it.

Well, well, well! It looked like the homeowner had punched a hole in the drywall for some reason, and rather than repair it, had put the register cover over it to camouflage the opening. Out of curiosity, I got out my moisture meter and checked the surrounding wall. No surprise there: the drywall was so wet it pegged the meter. But where was the water coming from?

The downspout was dumping water directly into the space at the base of the wall, where it infiltrated the foundation wall and penetrated all the way through to the interior wall. The homeowner likely tried to remedy the problem by punching a hole in the drywall to ventilate it, and put the grate up to make it look nicer while still allowing air circulation. Unfortunately, this wasn't enough to take care of the problem. The only solution was to extend the downspout so that rainwater drained six to ten feet away from the house.

About 85% of all water problems in the basement are directly attributable to gutters and downspouts. When I see downspouts draining at

That's not a return. What was the homeowner trying to accomplish here?

This downspout is dumping a considerable amount of water right at the foundation.

the foundation, I nearly always find some evidence of water infiltration at that corner.

Poor water management can impact so many things in and around a house. One of the less obvious problems is downspouts that drain right onto the driveway. When you're looking at the house on a dry day during the summer, it might not strike you as a particularly serious issue. But think about that same downspout during the winter, when snowmelt from the roof will flow down onto the driveway and freeze into a patch of ice, possibly causing injuries from falls or making vehicles skid.

Another issue with gutters is poorly-designed or poorly-installed gutter guards. While these are often marketed with big headlines promising "Never clean your gutters again!" the truth is that, even with guards, gutters need annual cleaning and maintenance to keep them in proper working order. We have seen guards that have collapsed into the gutter, blocking them completely. We've also seen gutters completely filled with decomposing leaves and debris, but since they had gutter guards, the owners assumed the didn't have to get them cleaned anymore.

Unsecured Hose Bibs

Two little screws. That's all it takes to secure a hose bib to the exterior of the house, yet so often they are missing. Securing the hose bibs is one of those five-minute jobs whose five minutes never seems to come up.

What's the big deal? Well, think of it this way. Imagine you're watering the lawn, and when you're done, you turn off the water at the hose bib. Only you want to make sure the water is shut off completely, so you twist the handle really, really hard. If the hose bib isn't fastened securely, all that twisting force could easily snap the water supply line inside the wall. Now you've got water gushing from a broken pipe inside the wall, causing a lot of expensive damage. Let's just hope you remember where the shutoff valves are inside the house before the basement floods!

Some builders slather the hose bib base with putty to prevent water or bugs from leaking into the opening. This often covers up the screw holes, so I'll carefully push the putty aside just enough to see if the screws are present... and they usually aren't. On brick facades, the bases are often simply set into a mortar bed, but that isn't correct either: screws must be used.

Holes in Trim

The outside of the house has one job: to keep the weather from getting in. Problems can occur at corners and intersections, so trim pieces help to bridge the gaps. These pieces are called fascia, rake, or frieze, depending upon which edge of the roof they are on. The trouble with these pieces is that they are prime targets for rot and critter damage.

Any time we see a hole in one of these trim pieces, we look carefully for signs of damage on the interior, usually in the form of a critter

This area where the sidewall intersected with two roof sections had been neglected for a long time, and the elements had significant deterioration and rot. This allowed holes to form and let water and critters into the walls.

infestation in the attic. We've seen it all: wasp nests, bird nests, even a bat colony.[10]

Modern houses tend to have lots of corners, angles, bumpouts, and dormers[11]. All of these create "plane intersections" - where two surfaces meet at an angle. Any time you have a corner, angle, or intersection, there's the opportunity for separation to happen, and water and critters to infiltrate.

With vinyl siding, the corners are typically covered with a pre-fabricated molded piece that extends from bottom to top in a single unit. The problem here is that the ends are often not sealed, which makes these trim corners like critter highways all the way up the side of the house, where there are likely overlooked gaps for them to get into the framing or attic.

EIFS

"Engineered Insulated Finishing Systems" (EIFS) became very popular in the 1970s, when the energy crisis made people more aware of the importance of energy-efficient houses. EIFS seemed like the perfect solution: it didn't require the installation skills that traditional stucco application did, and gave homeowners the lower energy bills they wanted.

Even a seemingly minor defect such as this in an EIFS exterior can lead to extensive interior damage.

---

10 See Chapter 19, "Environmental Hazards" for why this is a very bad thing to have.
11 Those extra little windows sticking out from the roof in the front of the house; in most new houses these are put in to give the illusion of living space in the top level, but they're just for show.

Unfortunately, the system only performed well if it was installed absolutely flawlessly: there could be no gaps, missing flashing, uncaulked openings, or any other defects. And it was very, very rarely installed perfectly. Any gaps, cracks, or other openings in the surface allowed water to penetrate into the framing, and since the system was specifically designed not to be breathable, any water that got in stayed in, and could cause horrendous damage that usually remained hidden. Only when the damage grew so extensive that it started affecting the interior surfaces would homeowners discover that the framing and sheathing of their homes had significant rot, leading to costly repairs (and lawsuits).

Home inspectors will typically disclaim EIFS. This means that they will note its presence and recommend the client contact a company that specializes in this type of cladding, but will not render any opinion on its condition. It's not that they are trying to "pass the buck;" so much of the damage from poorly-installed EIFS can be hidden, and requires evaluation by a trained EIFS expert. These inspections can take several days and cost several thousand dollars, and may involve destructive testing, but are the only way to get a complete and accurate picture of the condition of the framing and sheathing. What's worse, these inspections are supposed to be performed annually to catch problems before they lead to widespread damage.

To complicate the issue, there are new methods of EIFS installation that *do* have drainage planes behind them, and are able to drain the moisture safely away from behind the cladding (assuming it has been installed properly, that is). It is not always clear which method was used for a particular property, though, which is why we will typically advise our clients to get a specialist's opinion.

Here's more bad news: the same thing is happening to homes with Applied Stone Veneer Finishes (ASVF). Some builders refer to this stuff as "lick and stick." It's much like brick veneer, but usually lacks weep holes. This means water can't get out, and, like EIFS, the water can do tremendous damage to framing.

5
Decks

No Flashing

Decks are wonderful additions to homes. They allow you to enjoy the open air without worrying about muddy feet or uneven ground, and are great spots for entertaining. They can also be deadly.

The majority of decks use the structure of the house to support one or more of their sides. These edges have horizontal pieces called ledger boards, which are bolted to the side of the house. In most of the houses we inspect, this connection is done in such a way that eventual failure of the deck/house connection is almost a certainty.

Lumber is an organic material, and when it's exposed to the elements, it usually has an expected life of about 20 years. Even if it has been pressure-treated to resist damage from the elements, it is still prone to rot if not

This deck had seen much better days; the railing posts were severely rotted at the bottom, and there were sections that were leaning outward and looked like a stiff breeze would knock them down. I flagged the whole deck as a safety hazard.

properly protected. If the connection between the house and the deck fails, the result will be a deck collapse, which can lead to serious injury and even death. According to the CPSC, deck failures are occurring more and more often, increasing by more than 20% every year. And most of these could have been prevented with a thin piece of metal called flashing.

Flashing is what keeps the ledger board from coming into direct contact with the house. This helps prevent rot from developing and means the deck will be safe to use for much longer.[12]

The lifespan of a properly built and maintained deck is only around 15 years. Typically the first part to fail is the least visible: the fasteners. Lack of flashing can bathe the ledger bolts with moisture, causing them to corrode from the inside out. Once corrosion is visible on the exterior, the fastener has already lost a lot of its holding power, and the deck could fail a lot sooner.

Bad Railings

The function of a guardrail is to guard against falls. However, we see railings on decks that would not only fail to protect someone from a fall, but could actually cause someone to fall in the first place! Whenever I approach any kind of handrail on a stair or guardrail on a deck, it's almost

---

12   *But not indefinitely. Decks do have an average lifespan of around 15 years.*

second nature now for me to automatically give it a little shake to see if it's at all loose. It's amazing how few I find that are solid.

Guardrails are required when any walking surface has a height of 30 inches or more from grade. I always recommend guardrails if a fall from a particular location could result in injury, even if it's not 30 inches high.[13] These rails are supposed to withstand a point load of 200 pounds without deflecting more than half an inch; this simulates an adult stepping up to the rail and applying all their weight outward against it. When I'm doing inspections, I do what I call a "hip check" - that is, I stand perpendicular to the guardrail with my feet firmly planted, give the rail a swift nudge with my hip, and watch to see how much it moves.[14]

One of the problems is that people forget that decks are built with organic materials that won't last forever. Wood softens; moisture causes rot; fasteners corrode. Things loosen up over time. Decks really only have a lifespan of about 15 years, and it's the fasteners that fail first.[15]

Bad railings are one sign of a deck that might have been built without the proper permits and inspections from the local authorities. This can be bad news; see the chapter on "lack of permits" for more information.

Side-bolted Posts

There are many ways to build a deck, and a lot of them are wrong.

Decks weigh a lot. The wooden components themselves are heavy, and if you've got a party going, your guests could be adding several tons to the load. The average weight of an adult male in the United States is approaching 200 pounds, so if you and nine of your buddies are out on the deck, you could be adding as much as one ton to the load.

Now, imagine all those people standing in one corner of the deck. The load is now concentrated over one post. If that connection is not properly made, the deck could fail, collapsing under the load. This is a typical failure from side-bolted posts.

---

13 *A fall from two foot high porch onto a concrete driveway would still hurt. Put in a guardrail.*
14 *I shake it with my hand first; if it's really loose I'm not going to risk falling by doing the hip check.*
15 *This is assuming the deck was built properly in the first place.*

The beams supporting this deck are held up by just one bolt through the post. All the insect and woodpecker damage to the joist isn't a good sign either.

Decks must be constructed with proper load paths, just as houses are.[16] The weight of the deck is carried from the decking to the joists, then to the beams, then to the posts, and finally to the footing. A poor connection between any of these components can cause problems, but the worst is when a beam is not properly secured to the post. The most common poor connection here is a side-bolted beam.

Beams should rest solidly on the post, either on the flat top or in a notch. This provides a solid load path, but is difficult to get exactly right as it involves accurate measurement and cutting. It is much easier to simply drill a few holes through the beam and the post, insert some bolts, add some washers and nuts, and tighten them down.

So what's the big deal? Bolts are made of metal; they're thick, they're strong. What most people don't know is that bolts are meant to resist tensile force, not shear force. Tensile force is what wants to pull things apart. Shear force is what wants to slide things apart.

Side-bolting a beam means the bolt is being asked to resist forces it is not designed to withstand. The bolts will keep the beam from pulling away from the post, but if a large enough load is applied, those bolts will fail due to their lack of shear strength. The result is that the beam falls, taking the joists, decking, and occupants with it.

If the rest of the deck framing is in good shape, it's not difficult to fix this problem. There are special brackets that can be added to the framing that provide the needed support.

---

16 *More about this in an upcoming chapter about foundations.*

Fastened to a Cantilever

A cantilever is a section of framing that does not have any supports -- posts, piers or foundation -- directly beneath it. These suspended areas are not intended to bear any weight. Yet, we see decks fastened to them all the time.

Why is this such a bad thing? Well, a cantilever must be precisely engineered so that the suspended portion does not sag. This is done by making sure the joists that stick out over the foundation extend into the house framing at least twice as far as they stick out. This is called "backspan." and it is what gives the cantilever its support. It is counteracting the pull of gravity on the cantilever.

Now imagine hanging a lot of extra weight onto the cantilever. If the backspan is not designed to withstand it, there is a very real chance that the deck will collapse. The risks are even greater if the deck is overloaded. The joists will start to sag, and that could cause the ledger board to come loose from the house. Once that happens, gravity takes over, and the deck collapses towards the house.

The only way to repair this situation, short of replacing the deck, is to add support posts to take the weight of the deck where it meets the house. These should be designed and installed by a deck contractor, as the posts will need proper footings and need to be the right size for the job.

This deck is hanging from a cantilever along its entire length. Anyone sitting on the lower deck section will be crushed if the upper deck fails.

6
Roof

Moss

The typical asphalt shingle roof has an expected life of about 17 years. Once it has aged, it can't protect the house as well, leading to leaks and water damage. The amount of life left in a roof depends a lot upon multiple factors: exposure, climate, proper installation, and maintenance. Sometimes the signs of a failing roof can be subtle, but there is one that is highly visible: moss.

If I see mounds of green, puffy moss on a roof, I know that it is due for replacement. Unlike some surface growths, like algae or lichen, moss penetrates the shingles and can be a conduit for water to get through the sheathing and into the attic.

There are ways to prevent moss build-up on a roof: one common tactic is to install zinc along the ridge. Rain that hits these strips releases zinc carbonate, which is a fungistat, and as it runs down the roof, it prevents moss, algae, and fungus from growing. There are also chemicals that can be applied to remove moss, but by this time the damage has already been done.

The rule of thumb on shingle damage is that if 25% of the surface needs repair, it's time to replace the entire roof.

Curling or Buckling

Asphalt shingles have several layers. The base is a fiberglass mat, which is covered with asphalt, and topped with small granules. They are designed to shed water down the slope of the roof before it can penetrate the sheathing.

Over time, the granules lose their grip on the asphalt and get washed off. These granules are the "sunscreen" for the shingles, protecting them from ultraviolet radiation. It's like putting a coating of zinc oxide on your nose at the beach. Once this protection starts to wash away, sunlight can degrade the asphalt, causing it to dry out and deform the shingle base. This leads to one of the first signs of shingle failure: curling and buckling.

Curling is when the corners of the shingle tabs start lifting up. If the lift is severe enough, it can affect the roof drainage and allow water to get under the shingles. Buckling is when the rows of shingles get wavy, again preventing proper drainage. The only fix for these problems is replacement.

Stuff in Gutters

A properly designed and installed gutter system allows water to flow freely into the downspouts, to be carried away from the foundation. Debris in the gutter will prevent this free flow, and can cause a host of issues.

A common misconception is that having gutter guards installed means you never have to clean your gutters again. Actually, annual gutter cleaning is still recommended, as it's not just leaves that clog them. Other debris like shingle granules can get past the guards and block the rain from draining properly. As more water gets trapped, more debris can accumulate, causing a vicious cycle. The added weight of debris and standing water can cause gutters to pull away from the roof, exposing the framing to damage from

Most gutter guards are ineffective at preventing biuldup from evergreen needles such as Hemlock or White Pine.

water and critters. Eventually, the gutters will separate from the house; by this time, there is probably hidden damage inside the walls from water penetration.

Gutter cleaning is frequently done by homeowners, and may not be done as thoroughly as a professional would do. A proper cleaning job includes not just removing any debris from the gutters, but also clearing the downspouts, securing any sections of the system that have loosened, and replacing any damaged elements. If there are gutter guards in place, these will have to be removed to allow for complete cleaning, and then re-installed once the work is done.

It can be hard to look inside a gutter that has a solid "helmet" type of guard; sometimes all I can do is shine my flashlight through the narrow opening and get a glimpse of the interior. I rarely see a gutter with guards that doesn't have at least some debris inside it; I will always write these up as needing cleaning and regular maintenance.

Bad Gutters

"I've had a company come out to look at our damp basement and they tell me we need to install a $9,000 waterproofing system. Could you come out and take a look and give me your unbiased opinion?"

We get these calls a lot. So many people ask a company to come in and help them figure out what the problem is, only to find the company starts to do a very persuasive hard-sell on their particular product. In this case,

This concrete driveway sloped towards the house more than 3 inches over 8 feet. All that water was flowing right into the cracks at the house, causing a wet basement.

the client had removed some drywall from a basement corner as part of a remodeling project and found the wall to be a bit damp, with some dark streaks. They called a waterproofing company, which diagnosed the issue as hydrostatic water pressure from underneath the house, and told them they needed to put in an interior perimeter drain and a second sump crock and pump (there was an existing crock and pump not far from the problem area). They signed the contract but immediately felt they had made an error, and called us to see if we could come out the next day to take a look.

In talking with the client, I had a pretty good idea of what the problem was: a combination of bad drainage and bad gutters. Once I got to the house, my suspicions were confirmed. The driveway slab had subsided so it was now draining towards the foundation, and there was a gap between the driveway and the house that allowed the water easy access to flow down the foundation wall and penetrate to the interior. In addition, there were two downspouts that ended right at the foundation, which added even more water to the poorly-draining area.

Once I got inside and looked at the wall, I was able to reassure the client that the dark streaks on the wall were most likely not an organic growth, but rather rust from the nails used to fasten the wooden lath to the foundation blocks. Also, the existing sump crock was bone-dry; if the waterproofer's claim of subterranean water pressure was correct, the crock would always have some water in it.

The fix? Remove the concrete driveway slabs, properly regrade the soil, add slot drains to carry the excess water well away from the foundation, and pour a new driveway. The total cost would be less than the waterproofing,

Asphalt shingles shouldn't be used on such a low sloped roof. Water doesn't flow off fast enough, and can leak into the attic. The moss is also a sign of a roof at the end of its serviceable life.

and would actually fix the problem, rather than just dealing with a symptom[17].

Bad Choice of Material

Sometimes a roof can look great, but still be wrong because of which material was used as a covering. Certain materials are best used in specific applications or environments, and if they are used inappropriately, the life of the roof can be shorter than expected.

One example that we see all the time is asphalt shingles on a low slope roof. Shingles are designed to shed rainwater down to the gutters, and if that water can't flow fast enough because of the shallow angle of the roof, it can work its way under the shingles and penetrate the house. Fixing this issue requires removal of the shingles, repair of any damaged framing, and applying a covering more suited for a low slope (such as roll roofing).

Asphalt shingles are best for roofs with a slope that rises at least 4 feet for every 12 feet in length (called a 4/12 slope). It may also be used on a shallower roof, down to 2/10, if it has a waterproof membrane installed underneath that extends all the way from the eave to the ridge. Unfortunately, this is something that is not readily visible during a home inspection, so I advise my client to request the documentation on the roof if it's available to determine whether it was installed properly.

---

17   *And they would just have had to fix the driveway slope problem eventually anyway.*

Sometimes the issue isn't that the slope is wrong for the material, but that the material is wrong for the climate. In the southwestern parts of the United States, clay tile roofs are very popular, and their durability and ventilating properties make them a good choice for that hot, dry climate. But take that same clay tile and install it on a roof in northern Michigan, and it will start to deteriorate quickly; the clay absorbs moisture well, which will make it susceptible to shattering during the winter.

Don't assume that a tile roof in a cold climate is installed incorrectly, though; there are special tiles made of cold-resistant materials, so if that style of roof is appealing, you can have it on your house no matter where you live.[18]

Whenever new roofing is installed, especially when changing the type, pay attention to whether the roof framing is strong enough to support it. Some materials, like slate, are incredibly heavy, and the framing must be designed for it. All roof framing is engineered to withstand a certain load, and if that is exceeded, the framing can buckle and collapse.

---

18   *Keep in mind, though, that a clay roof can be very expensive to install properly, and requires periodic maintenance to keep it in good shape.*

Notes from the Field

Home Inspectors are often asked, "What's the wierdest thing you've found during an inspection?" This is the one that has always stood out for me.

Even though we are not required to inspect sheds, I will typically take a quick look inside one if it is unlocked, mostly to confirm that there are no utilities such as electric or phone lines supplying it. I usually find normal stuff like mowers, garden tools, and yard toys. But this time...

Yes, that is indeed an Emmy Award statuette. I took a picture of the engraved label on it and looked it up when I got back to the office. It was authentic! I have no idea why it was in such an odd place. It just goes to show that my job can be full of surprises!

7
Foundation

Horizontal Cracks

Horizontal cracks, especially in block foundations, can signal big problems with the structural integrity of the house. In order to understand why, it's important to have a grasp of the basic forces acting on a structure.

One concept to cover before getting into structural cracking is that of load. We're all familiar with gravity; it's what is pulling everything on the planet directly downward towards the core of the Earth. Your house is also being pulled downward, along with everything in it.

There are two types of load on a house: dead load and live load. Dead load is the static weight of the house: the wood framing, the windows, the roof trusses, the shingles. All of these don't really change much over time. Live load is everything else: the furniture, the people, the appliances, the two feet of snow that fell during the last blizzard. Houses are constructed to withstand a specified amount of dead and live load; it's usually more than enough to stay standing even under extreme conditions.

But there's another force at play: lateral (sideways) load. This is the weight of the earth piled up against the foundation, of the water that's contained in that soil, and also of the wind howling during a storm. These forces can wreak a lot of damage on a house.

Say there is a lot of water draining at the foundation of the house (usually due to bad gutters or poor grading). This water gets into the soil piled against the house, and starts exerting pressure against the foundation walls. In the winter, this water will freeze and exert even more pressure. Eventually, the foundation succumbs to this pressure, and develops a crack. This is now a weak spot, and unless the matter is corrected, the wall will start to bow inwards. If the bowing gets too bad, the wall will no longer have a proper load path for the weight of the house above it, and there is a real risk of collapse.

Only a structural engineer will be able to determine whether a crack presents a major threat to a house. Getting an engineer's opinion will usually run about $500.

Cracks Wider than 1/4"

We see a lot of cracks in poured concrete foundations. Most of them are not structurally significant; with very narrow cracks, the only real issue is water penetration. We usually recommend having these cracks sealed with

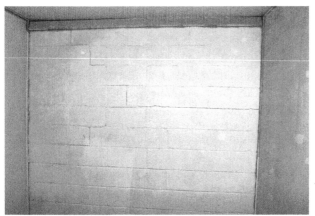

Horizontal crack on a concrete masonry block foundation wall. You can see the crack extending to the top and bottom of the corner; this indicates significant hydrostatic pressure on the other side, pushing the whole wall in.

a flexible material like polyurethane by a company that will issue a warranty against future leakage at that location.

But what about bigger cracks? Generally, if a crack is wider than one quarter inch, or if it has signs of movement in more than one plane, it indicates a problem.

Say you've got a crack running vertically in the wall, and it's a quarter inch wide along its entire width. If we didn't see any evidence of problems in the upper floors above the area of the crack, we would probably recommend having it sealed, and monitoring it for any future movement.

How about if the crack is a bit wider at one end? Again, it depends upon whether there are signs of movement elsewhere in the house. If the difference isn't enormous, and there are no other warning signs, monitoring might still be the proper action. Even so, we make sure the client understands that only an engineer has the training to completely analyze the situation and render a professional opinion.

Now imagine that that same crack is not only a quarter inch wide at the bottom and an inch wide at the top, but one side is sticking out more than the other. Now there's movement in two planes, and there could be something more serious going on. We would recommend consulting an engineer in cases like this, just to help identify any potential structural issues.

If we also see that one side of that crack has not only moved horizontally but also vertically, there is now movement in three planes, and

The white stuff isn't soap suds, or organic growths; it's efflorescence. That plus the stains suggest persistent water intrusion through this foundation wall.

there is definitely something bad happening to the foundation. Time to get that engineer on site!

Water and Efflorescence

In an unfinished basement, it's common to see white or gray material sticking to the inside of the walls, especially in corners or in places where the ground outside is especially wet. Some people immediately worry that it is organic growth, but it usually isn't; it's a mineral buildup called efflorescence[19].

Water is a great solvent. It picks up impurities as it passes through materials and carries them onward as it flows. When the water stops flowing, the particles sink and build up along the path of travel. If the water evaporates, the particles are left behind, clinging to whatever surface they landed on.

Concrete is porous; this is why foundation walls are given a waterproof coating called parging on the outside before backfilling. Without this parging, moisture from the soil would readily soak through the foundation and into the house. Gaps or imperfections in the parging allow some water to get through, and as it does, it picks up mineral salts from the concrete to go along with whatever impurities it was already carrying. When the water finally reaches the interior side of the foundation, it evaporates, leaving all these tag-along materials behind. This is efflorescence.

In most cases, efflorescence is just a nuisance. It can cause paint to slough off the interior of a basement wall, and can cause ugly staining. The only way to stop it completely is to either prevent the water from getting into the foundation in the first place, or to make sure it doesn't evaporate on the surface. Keeping the water out means excavating around the house and applying new waterproofing materials and drainage systems; this is a very expensive proposition, but if the moisture issue is bad enough it might be necessary. A less costly solution is to make sure the foundation is as dry as possible on the inside, either with a dehumidifying system or with good ventilation. If the interior surface of the foundation is kept dry, any moisture penetrating the walls will evaporate before reaching the surface, keeping the impurities inside the wall instead of letting them build up on the outside.

19   From French, "to flower out."

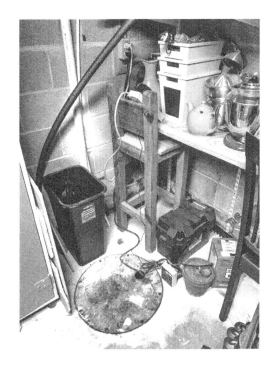

Sump pump, with battery backup and a water alarm (the little box right at the edge of the sump crock cover), added during an interior waterproofing job. The sump outlet pipe drained right at the foundation wall, so it was constantly having to pump out the same water.

If you look just behind the battery box, you will see the top of the black drainage mat sticking up between the basement floor slab and the foundation wall.

Multiple Sump Pumps

Sump crocks and pumps are common features in most new construction. Just having one doesn't mean the house has a moisture issue; most builders install them as a matter of routine because it's much easier to have one in place in case it's needed, rather than to put one in after the fact.

If a house without an existing sump crock experiences a water problem, many homeowners opt to have an interior perimeter drain installed by a waterproofing company. This involves excavating a trench around the inside of the foundation wall, installing drainage material and piping, and connecting these pipes to a sump crock with a pump in it to send the accumulated water back outside. It's pretty easy to spot this type of system in an unfinished basement: look for the black drainage material along the perimeter of the basement floor slab.

The issue with these systems is that they are treating the symptom, rather than the cause. Once the water has gotten through the foundation and into the house, it has already damaged the foundation materials. To make matters worse, much of the time the sump pump outlet pipe dumps the water right against the foundation, so it can work its way inside again. It's a vicious cycle.

One sump pump is common. It's more of a concern when there are multiple crocks and pumps in various locations in the basement. This can point to a more severe and chronic water problem. If possible, you should lift the cover of a crock and look inside to see whether there is any standing water, or if it looks like it is persistently wet. A sump system installed during construction as a precaution is typically dry and clear; one that gets a lot of use may look slimy and muddy.

Another telltale sign of persistent water issues is if you see battery backups on the sump systems, along with spare pumps nearby. This typically means the occupants have learned from experience that the sump pumps must be operational, even during power outages, and that when they fail, they must be replaced immediately.[20]

The owners insulated the foundation walls of this crawl space, thinking it would help with the moisture problem. However, they left the vents open, so the space stayed very wet.

---

20   *As I tell my clients, sump pumps never fail when it's bright and sunny and the hardware stores are open.*

Musty Crawl Spaces

Crawl spaces with dirt floors are often neglected spaces. Homeowners tend to ignore them, or will sometimes even seal the access hatch or the vent openings. Many times, I'm the first person to go into the crawl space in years, so it's no wonder these spaces tend to smell pretty bad.

Why do some home have crawl spaces, anyway? They aren't suitable for living space, but some people do use them for storage. This is usually not a good idea, since the temperature and humidity swings will cause anything[21] stored in them to deteriorate quickly.

Crawl spaces are meant to raise the first level of the house enough so that moisture won't get in and rot the framing. They can be anywhere from a foot deep to nearly standing height, although once they get to a height where I can walk (albeit hunched over), I start calling them cellars.

There are two ways to build a crawl space: unconditioned, and conditioned. Which is done where you are depends upon the local standards and common building practices, but in older homes the crawl spaces were typically unconditioned.

Unconditioned crawl spaces are considered "outside the envelope" of the house. That is, they don't have a means to condition the air, and often have insulation against the "ceiling" of the crawl space, which is the underside of the first floor. They also have vents open to the outside to provide fresh air and give the humidity a way to escape. These crawl spaces usually have dirt floors, sometimes covered with a plastic vapor barrier to try and reduce the moisture coming up from the ground.

On the other hand, conditioned crawl spaces are "inside the envelope," so they have ductwork and registers or other methods to supply fresh air to the space. They typically have insulation applied to the exterior walls, no exterior vents, and either heavy plastic well-sealed at the seams to cover the dirt floor, or a solid concrete slab floor. Conditioned crawl spaces are ideal for storage, since they're not going to be subject to the environmental changes that unconditioned crawl spaces are.

---

21 *Especially plastics and photographs. You may also find that rubber deteriorates rapidly when stored in unconditioned space.*

8
Structure and Framing

Broken or Altered Trusses

In traditional construction, roof framing consists of rafters and ceiling joists, creating an attic with large open spaces that were used for storage. These framing elements were cut on site, requiring a lot of skill and creating a lot of waste lumber. This created a bottleneck in production in the postwar building boom, until the invention of premanufactured roof trusses in 1952.

Roof trusses are made by laying out pieces of two-by-four lumber according to a pattern specified by an architect or engineer for a particular location in a roof, putting galvanized steel gusset plates at each intersection, and pressing the assembly under thousands of pounds of pressure to embed the plates into the wood and hold everything together. The whole truss is then raised onto the house and secured into place. This allows a construction crew to frame a roof in a matter of hours, rather than days.

Trusses do have one extremely important limitation: they cannot be modified unless an engineer says the change is not going to compromise the structural integrity of the roof. This means they should never be cut, bored, trimmed, or altered in any way. If they are, they must be repaired according to the manufacturer's specifications.[22]

I have seen trusses cut for lots of reasons: putting in a pull-down attic stair assembly, adding a furnace or air handler, or even in an attempt to make the attic more "usable." Doing any of these things can cause significant structural problems that could lead to catastrophic roof failure.

The only time I can really get a good look at the condition of the roof trusses is during a pre-drywall inspection. I spend a lot of time on the upper level, my head tilted back, scanning every truss to check for damaged elements or missing gusset plates.[23] I photograph any problems for my report and advise my client that all of those issues must be repaired according to the manufacturer's instructions, which includes documenting each repair and giving this paperwork to the owner. Ideally, I like to see a copy of the paperwork stapled to the repair itself, but this step is often omitted.

Just because a roof has traditional framing doesn't mean you're free to make changes. I inspected one home, built in the 1880s, where the previous owner had removed the collar ties between the rafters in order to turn the attic into usable space. These ties have a crucial job: to prevent the rafters from collapsing, or spreading outward.

FRT Plywood Sheathing

In the 1980s there was an enormous increase in housing construction, particularly for higher-density units like townhomes. This type of property has to have fire protection to reduce the risk of fire spreading from one unit to another, ideally with masonry walls between the units extending from the foundation all the way up to the top of the roof. But this is a time-consuming and costly construction method, so builders sought to speed

---

22 *These specifications are never as simple as "just nail them back together."*
23 *I have yet to leave a pre-drywall inspection without a very sore neck.*

The rich mahogany color of this sheathing is a sign that it is deteriorated FRT plywood. It should be replaced with modern treated sheathing.

things up, which led to the introduction of fire retardant treated (FRT) plywood.

FRT plywood is impregnated with chemicals to make it less flammable. This is done under pressure, much like exterior-grade pressure-treated lumber, driving the chemicals through the layers of plywood. By using FRT plywood for roof sheathing, along with different framing methods for party walls, builders were able to eliminate the need for masonry fire walls. This sped up construction and reduced costs.

Unfortunately, reports started surfacing in the late 1980s of roof failures in homes with FRT plywood. In some cases, the sheathing became so brittle that a person walking across the roof could cause it to give way. This turned out to be due to some of the chemicals used in the treatment process: they attacked the lignin in the wood, which caused the layers to weaken and start separating, called delamination.

FRT plywood is often recognized by its color: the heat of the attic makes the wood look almost charred, and it turns a deep mahogany. If I suspect plywood is FRT, I will put my hand against it and push hard: FRT will often flex under the pressure, and will make a very distinctive crunchy noise.

Unfortunately, the only fix for FRT is complete removal and replacement with newer materials that are treated with newer fire retardants that do not damage wood. I have seen houses with brand-new shingles installed over FRT plywood, and have to give the bad news that the roof will need to be completely redone.

Critters or Droppings

While doing my walk-around of a house before going inside, I pay special attention to the areas where the side of the house meets the roof. If I see gaps or holes, there's the possibility that critters have made their way into the attic. So before I open the attic access, I will knock on the cover or rattle it to make noise, to hopefully scare any occupants away.

I've seen all sorts of animals living in attics: mice, squirrels, birds, bats, snakes, and even raccoons. These pests can damage framing, they make noise, and their droppings can contain pathogens. Anything living in an attic must be removed; in the case of protected species like bats or flying squirrels, this must be done by a wildlife specialist who can do it without harming them.

Bats are beneficial insect-eating creatures and should never be killed. If you have bats in your attic, call a wildlife removal company to have them safely relocated.

Once the invaders are removed and their access points sealed up, all of the affected materials must be removed as well. This includes any nesting materials brought in by the animal, as well as insulation and drywall contaminated with droppings or urine. In cases where the animal created tunnels in the insulation, it may be necessary to remove all the insulation to ensure there are no remaining droppings. This isn't something to take lightly: rodents are known to carry all sorts of exotic diseases such as hantavirus, which can become airborne when feces are disturbed.

It doesn't take a big opening to let critters into the house. Mice can fit through holes about the diameter of a pencil. Squirrels can chew through almost anything to make their own access. Bats will climb up the wall and slip through gaps between pieces of siding. And bugs... well, let's just say there's a reason why we always recommend good caulking around any kind of penetration!

Once you know what to look for, the signs of infestation are pretty easy to spot. Look for chewed holes in the trim, streaks of droppings down the siding, or twigs poking out of holes. Eradication of critters may require working with a trapper, since some species (like bats) are beneficial, and shouldn't be killed. Just remember that we are the interlopers on their territory!

Bearing Walls Altered

It was a lovely little cottage near a lake. "Completely remodeled," the listing said. Indeed, it looked great, with a bright, open floor plan on the first level. But as I was walking through the house at the start of the inspection, something didn't feel quite right. On the second floor, there seemed to be a bit of a dip in the floor.

Uneven floors aren't that unusual in century-old houses, but this one was relatively new. I went back to the first level to see what was under the dip, and saw that it was over the open space between the kitchen and living room. This open space was in the middle of the house, directly over the main beam in the basement. Uh oh...

Remember load paths? In houses with truss framing, much of the weight is borne by exterior walls and perimeter foundation, which allows builders a lot of flexibility in creating open spaces inside. But in traditional framing, the load is distributed throughout the house, via bearing walls, beams, and columns. Altering any of those elements changes the way the load is carried, and if the change is done without calculating those changes and accounting for them, the result can be structural collapse.

In this little cottage, the kitchen used to be walled off from the main room, with an opening on each end. This was typical for most houses built before the 1980s; kitchens were functional spaces, not showplaces. But many buyers want open, gourmet kitchens even in old houses, so the renovators[24] updated this home's interior by removing the wall between the two rooms and creating the new open space, apparently without bothering to check whether the wall was doing anything important, like holding up the house.

In home inspection, one of the things that's hardest to spot is something that isn't there. Sometimes the only way to identify a missing structural element is by noticing the effect on other components in the house. It could be a dip in the floor, or a sag in the roof, or a bouncy

See that rust stain on the underside of the I-beam? That's where a structural steel post used to be attached. The homeowner was in the process of refinishing the basement and didn't want the post there, so he just removed it. If the drywall had been finished, it would be hard to spot this... until the floor above started to sag.

---

24   *Yep, they were flippers.*

floor. All of these symptoms can mean changes were made to the load path of the house, and a structural engineer will have to come in and make an assessment of how bad the damage is, and how it should be repaired. And fixing structural issues is rarely a quick and easy proposition.

One of the worst things people do is try to move steel columns in a basement. Sure, they're usually right in the middle of a big open area, and if you just moved it a couple of feet over it would make the space so much nicer. It shouldn't matter, because you'll keep it under the beam, right?

Nope. The column's position is determined by the engineers who calculated the load path for that house. There's a footing under that column that is designed to carry the load to ground. Moving a column off the footing means the load is now being carried by the thin floor slab, which has no structural strength even though it feels pretty solid when you walk across it. The result can be that the weight of the house will eventually punch that column through the slab, causing the entire house to dip down and threatening the stability of the whole structure.

It's certainly possible to move bearing walls and columns, but the whole process must be designed and specified by a structural engineer after analyzing the present structure. Structural changes almost always require building permits and municipal inspections. The contractors must follow the drawings precisely, and all the paperwork should become a part of the house's documentation so that any future owners will know it was done properly.

As for the little cottage, my clients decided to pass on buying it because of the possibility of facing huge expenses to fix the structural problems. They happily paid for me to inspect their next house too, and left a nice online review as well. Sometimes my happiest clients are the ones I've saved from buying a money pit.

9
Interior Surfaces

Sagging Ceilings

Ceilings should be flat. A ceiling that is not flat has a problem. It really is that simple.

Most houses have drywall ceilings (and walls). Drywall is made of gypsum, which is calcium sulfate dihydrate with some additives and binders, compressed between two pieces of paper. Unlike concrete or plaster, when drywall gets wet, it will dissolve.

Drywall is typically screwed to the wall studs and ceiling joists, sometimes with adhesive added for good measure. The thickness of the drywall, spacing of the framing, and the number and type of fasteners are calculated during the design process, and if any of these variables aren't correct, the result can be a sagging ceiling.

Ceilings that have gotten wet, either from a leak above them or just really high humidity in the room, are the most prone to sagging. The paper backing soaks up the water, the gypsum gets saturated and starts to soften, and the fasteners lose their holding power. In extreme cases, the drywall can fall off completely.

Sagging ceilings can be repaired, but if the damage is too severe, the drywall should be removed to ensure there is no structural damage behind it.

One thing to watch out for is when homeowners cover up a sagging ceiling issue by installing a new ceiling below it, usually as a suspended ceiling tile system. While my state's Standards of Practice don't require me to lift up ceiling tiles to look behind them, I will usually try to do so, especially if I have seen other evidence of shoddy work in the house.

While hanging drywall isn't particularly difficult, it is one of those projects that may be better left to professionals. Lifting sheets of drywall over your head and holding them up to fasten them is extremely tiring; after all, it's made of rock!

Something to be aware of is that once drywall has gotten wet, it will need to be replaced. The compressed powder that makes up the material will absorb water and will never have the same strength or smoothness.

Corner Cracks

Houses are made of organic materials like wood framing, that react to changes in temperature and humidity by swelling and shrinking. However, the materials that cover the framing are typically inorganic, like drywall, which don't have the same flexibility. So if the shape of the wood underneath the wall changes, the result can be cracks.

Just like with foundations, cracks in interior walls have varying degrees of structural significance. Most of the cracks we see are shrinkage cracks, caused by the normal variations in the wood framing. Others can point to more serious issues, sometimes in places that aren't directly behind the cracks.

Here's the problem: a lot of the clues are hidden inside the walls. We can't always see whether a crack is confined to one area, or if it extends

This crack could indicate movement in the foundation, or it could just be sloppy drywall. It's important to evaluate all the clues before drawing conclusions.

further, because we can't poke a hole in the wall to follow it up or down. But there are little hints that we can spot that will lead us to recommend having a structural engineer pay a visit.

For example, if I see a crack in the foundation while I'm walking around outside, I will note where it is and look very carefully in the areas above that crack on the interior surfaces. If there is evidence that the crack has "telegraphed" - that is, if I can see cracks that follow the same lines as the ones I saw on the outside - then it becomes more urgent to get an engineer to evaluate the property and render an expert opinion.

When looking at any crack, it's important to think in three dimensions. Every plane of movement increases the structural severity of a crack, no matter where it's located. Corner cracks are a bit of a special case, though: they're supposed to be the strongest part of the wall, so cracks in that area mean there could be some serious movement happening somewhere.

Sometimes the problem may be as simple as sloppy drywall work, and what looks like a crack is just the corner tape rippling or pulling away. But if there are signs of movement - like the ceiling trim no longer lines up, or there is a slope in the floor, or you notice a door that isn't square in the frame, you could be looking at a problem.

If we see enough clues, we will recommend bringing in a structural engineer to analyze the house and determine if the structure has been compromised, and specify a fix. Depending upon the cause, the fix might be simple bracing, or could be as complex as jacking up the house and rebuilding the foundation. Whatever the findings, it's important to get the complete picture of what's going on inside your walls.

Bowed Walls

In most houses, walls are vertical and straight. We do occasionally see curved walls, but these are typically in older homes with plaster finishes, and it's obvious that the bends are intentional. When a drywall interior surface isn't flat, it's not a good sign.

The exterior wall on this house is anything but straight and plumb! It's not clear whether the first and second floors are pushing out, or the framing is collapsing in. Whichever is the case, this will require the input of a structural engineer to determine the cause, and specify the fix. Whatever it is, you can be sure it will be an expensive repair!

Houses are subject to a lot of different forces. You might think gravity is the biggest concern, but it actually isn't. A bigger issue is lateral forces: the ones that push and pull a house sideways. As long as the walls are plumb and square, they are doing the job of transferring the weight of the house and its contents to the footings, resisting gravity and keeping the house up.

But if those walls start to lean, that load transfer is interrupted. The force of gravity doesn't just stop, though; it keeps pushing downward. If the leaning is bad enough, the wall collapses. The same holds true for bowing walls; the load path, or the downward force of gravity, is a vertical line, and if that line falls far enough outside the structural member, gravity takes over and the member can fail.

Bowed walls are a sign that lateral forces aren't being properly controlled. In old houses, this can sometimes be seen as a bulge right at the second floor level. This is typically due to the failure of the connection between the floor joists and the building's exterior. The joists don't just hold up the floorboards: their job is also to resist the outward movement of the exterior walls.

A common feature on some old house exteriors is cast iron ornaments, typically star-shaped, visible from the outside at the level of the second floor framing. These aren't just quaint decorations; they are structural tiebacks, and are connected in pairs on opposite sides of a structure with two very long threaded rods between them that are joined with a turnbuckle. These are literally holding the sides of the house in. If they are removed, structural failure is a very real possibility.

Inspection Tales
by Welmoed Sisson, Inspections by Bob

"'Allo, Guv'na! I'm 'ere from the Chim-Chim-Cheree Chimney Sweep Company!"

©2018 Inspections by Bob, LLC

10
Fireplace and Chimney

Damaged/missing bricks

You can tell a lot about the health of a fireplace system by looking at the exterior of the chimney. Is it leaning? Is it separating from the house? Is it cracking? Does it have a rain cap and spark screen? And are there missing or damaged bricks and/or mortar?

You may think that these issues aren't that serious, but when it comes to chimneys, almost any damage is a potential fire hazard.[25] The problems above aren't simply cosmetic; they are evidence of water damage inside the body of the chimney, which can cause gaps in the flue (especially if it's clay tile). Gaps can allow smoke and hot ash to escape the flue, and if those gaps are in an area where the chimney passes through or next to the house, the result can be a catastrophic house fire.

25   *It's why I'm so insistent about a Level II inspection by a certified chimney sweep.*

This family was extremely lucky: a neighbor spotted the smoke billowing from the roof and called the fire department.

A few years ago, I saw fire trucks pulling into our neighborhood and stopping just a few blocks away. I went over to see what was going on, and one of the firefighters told me a neighbor had noticed smoke billowing from the roof. The family escaped safely, and the fire crew discovered an attic fire, which was determined to have originated from the chimney. Fortunately, the damage wasn't severe, thanks to the neighbor's action.

Water can do a lot of damage to a brick chimney. Bricks are porous, so they can be seriously affected when water soaks into them and then freezes. The ice expands, but the bricks can't, so the ice pushes outward and causes the surface of the brick to slough off. This is called spalling, and it's a common defect on brick surfaces. This spalling can happen to the interior of the chimney as well.

One of the leading causes of interior chimney spalling is lack of a rain cap. All chimneys should have a solid metal cap that covers the entire flue to prevent rain water from penetrating the interior.

Water Stains

During my inspection, I will look inside the fireplace and check its condition. Most of the time, I won't be able to see much beyond the damper, but I might get a glimpse of the throat and beginning of the flue.

This type of inspection won't tell the whole story about the health of the fireplace system; for that you need to get a Level II inspection from a certified chimney sweep[26] (for more details, see Chapter 19: When to Call a Specialist).

One of the main things I look for inside the fireplace is water damage. This shows up as streaks and stains along the back and sides, along with spalling and cracking of the firebrick. This is a sign that water has penetrated somewhere along the chimney system and worked its way down, so there's a pretty good chance that there is damage I can't see.

A proper fireplace and chimney system is smooth and clear, with minimal creosote buildup. If you look inside a fireplace and it is caked with shiny black goo, you should not start any fires in it until it has been cleaned and completely inspected. Otherwise you run the risk of having a chimney fire, since creosote can ignite.

The typical entry point for water in a chimney system is the crown at the top. The flat top surface of the chimney needs to be able to shed rainwater, so it is usually capped with a concrete or metal top. Because this part of the chimney is rarely seen, it's easy to lose track of whether it is in good shape[27]. Once a crown develops cracks and gaps, water makes its way into the flue and starts damaging the masonry.

Staining on the inside of the firebox is a sign of water penetration, often from way up at the top of the chimney.

---

26   *I always recommend using one who is a member of CSIA, the Chimney Safety Institute of America (csia.org).*

27   *I've only seen maybe half a dozen chimney crowns that were in decent condition. Most are in dire need of repair.*

Signs of water damage to a chimney system can be identified by rust on the damper, or on other metal components. If there is any damage at all, it's prudent not to use the fireplace until it can be inspected and repaired.

Cracked/Loose Firebrick

The inside of the fireplace must be able to withstand a lot of heat, which is why it is constructed with special bricks that are joined with fireproof mortar. Any breaks or gaps in these materials can allow heat, smoke, embers, or even flames to escape the firebox and cause a house fire.

There should be no gaps or cracks at all anywhere inside the firebox. If there are, the fireplace should not be used at all until they are repaired. Repairs need to be done by masonry contractors, using the correct materials.[28]

When I'm looking inside the firebox, I pay special attention to the condition of the brick and mortar. Any kind of cracking, missing mortar,

This chimney cap is in seriously bad condition. Over time, water seeped into the concrete and bricks and, when it froze, simply caused the materials to disintegrate.

---

28   *I've seen homeowner repairs done with questionable materials and always mark them as a significant defect.*

Extensive staining and cracking in a firebox, along with evidence of prior repair attempts, will lead me to mark the fireplace as unsafe to use until inspected and repaired by a chimney specialist.

or damage to the bricks. Sometimes my view is blocked; although I'm not required to move anything to look behind them, I will move stuff if I think an effort has been made to conceal a problem (yes, it happens!).

Repairs to firebrick are expensive. In fact, any repair to a fireplace or chimney is expensive! It's not that the work is particularly difficult; the issue is that getting at the area that needs repair can involve scaffolding, safety equipment, or having to remove sections of the masonry. Many times, too, even issues like they should be fairly easy to fix, such as missing mortar or damaged bricks, cannot simply be patched. Because of the very real potential for catastrophic fire damage, chimneys will often have to be completely demolished all the way down to the damaged portion, and then rebuilt. So if the damage is down near the base of the chimney, you could be facing a complete replacement, which could easily exceed $25,000 or more.

Missing Damper

A wood-burning fireplace is essentially a big open tube in the house, pulling air out. This is called the "stack effect." It is one of the major avenues of energy loss in a home, so chimneys have heavy iron or steel flaps that can be closed when the fireplace is not in use to help prevent air from being sucked up into it.

Often people will leave the damper open even if the fireplace isn't being used. This may happen because they forget to close the damper after the fire has gone out. Or, the damper is always open because they don't want to reach up into a dark, sooty space and wrestle with the mechanism to close it. Sometimes the damper is so corroded it can't be closed, or is missing entirely.

Part of my fireplace inspection is operating the damper. This can sometimes have unpleasant consequences: I often get a shower of soot and debris raining down on my hand when I open a damper that's been closed for a very long time. Or worse: an unused chimney is prime real estate for various critters: raccoons, birds, squirrels, bees, and wasps. If I see any signs of animal occupancy when I open the damper, I close it immediately and recommend a complete cleaning and inspection of the interior.

Sometimes the damper itself is the hazard. Many older masonry fireplaces have been modified with gas log inserts, to allow the ambiance of a cozy fire without hauling the logs or cleaning up ashes. Just like any gas-burning appliance, these must be vented to the outdoors, even when they're not being used. A damper blocks that venting, so a device must be installed on the damper to prevent it from closing completely. This means there will always be energy loss through the chimney, and an avenue for water and critters to get into the house. In our own home, we had a gas insert installed in one of the fireplaces, and noticed that we were suddenly getting a lot of wasps in the house. Sure enough, they were coming through the gap in the damper. This is why I now recommend that any such fireplace get a tightly-fitting glass door covering the hearth opening.

No Rain Cap/Spark Screen

The top of the chimney is exposed to the elements. Rain falls, leaves swirl, and it can all end up inside an unprotected chimney. If you look up at the top of a chimney and see just the flue sticking out, the potential for hidden damage inside is very real.

Chimney exteriors must be able to shed water efficiently; it should not simply run down the exterior. The best chimneys have a cap extending beyond the edge, to direct rain away from the outside. This method, when used in conjunction with a good rain cap, helps prolong the life of the entire chimney system. Unfortunately, the trend these days is to simply apply a layer of mortar across the top of the chimney, called a Cement Wash. This top treatment usually deteriorates rapidly, allowing water to get inside the flue, and it also means the rain dripping off the top of the chimney will run down the sides, clinging to the brick and mortar and hastening their deterioration. If there are any minuscule cracks in the exterior, the water will get inside and start spalling the bricks.

Any functional fireplace needs a rain cap to keep the rain out. This is usually a flat metal assembly, mounted on a metal frame that usually includes a spark screen to prevent any embers that are swept up the flue from escaping and landing on the roof. Many times these two elements are damaged or blown off during storms, or are omitted entirely. Any time I see a chimney without either of these elements, I know that there's a good chance the inside of the firebox is going to have at least some water damage, and the damper might be rusted as well.

Here's the thing about chimney and fireplace issues: they are expensive to repair. It's not that the work is complicated; it's because the components are covered by a lot of brick. Installing a rain cap and spark screen is pretty simple, but getting to the top of the chimney could require scaffolding, or a a bucket truck, and safety equipment to protect from falls. If a damper needs to be replaced, that's going to be much more complicated, since it's a

All three of these flues are completely unprotected from water damage. Embers could escape and cause fires. What's more, the chimney crown is eroded and has exposed the cored bricks used to build the chimney; these cores are another pathway for water intrusion.

very tight work space and replacing the damper might require demolishing the inside of the fireplace to get it into place. This is why we encourage buyers to get a questionable fireplace professionally inspected by a chimney sweep with the right equipment to see all the components[29] and to get an estimate for the repair cost before heading to the closing table.

No Clearance to Combustibles

Crackling wood fires are both romantic and hazardous. The moisture inside the logs turns into steam, which can erupt through the surface, sending burning embers flying. If one of those embers lands on a combustible surface, it can start a fire somewhere other than inside the fireplace.

A wood-burning masonry fireplace should have some sort of protective metal screen in front of it to prevent embers from flying out. It should also not have anything combustible anywhere near the opening of the fireplace. There should be a fireproof floor extending at least 16 inches in front and 8 inches to each side (more for a large opening). The wall surrounding the fireplace opening should also be covered with non-combustible materials for at least 8 inches. The whole idea is to not give any stray embers a chance to cause unintended fires.

Chimneys themselves must also not be in contact with any combustible elements; there should be at least two inches of clearance. Exhaust from a fire makes chimneys quite hot, and if wood is exposed to this heat it can undergo a chemical change called pyrolysis. This change lowers the ignition point of the wood, so it takes less heat to make it burst into flame. Wood that has undergone pyrolysis will darken, but it is not uncommon for this to be mistaken for water damage.

It is important to remember that anything hanging from or otherwise attached to a mantle also needs to be kept well away from the fireplace opening. The stockings may be hung with care, but if they are hanging too close to the fire, they could ruin Christmas. The same goes for festive garlands and other decorations; keep them well away from the heat and flames.

---

29   Typically with a remote camera lowered down the flue.

Notes from the Field

One of the more "interesting" houses I've seen had this unusual setup in the master bedroom. The rolling ladder led to a loft room, and on the other side of the loft was a door leading to a utility room which held the HVAC equipment for the indoor pool.

The house was big enough that Bob and I inspected it as a team. He was doing the mechanical systems in the basement while I was working on this area of the house. I scaled the ladder and carefully maneuvered myself onto the loft floor (there were no grab bars or rails). As I left the ladder, my leg swung against it, which caused it to roll away from the opening.

It came to a stop out of reach of the opening. The bookcases flanking the loft entrance prevented me from reaching the ladder to pull it back. I was stuck.

I called out for Bob but this was a very large house and he was out of earshot. Ah, but I had my cell phone with me! However, Bob was in the habit of turning his off during inspections. I had to resort to waiting for him to wonder where I was and come find me.

After he stopped laughing, he rolled the ladder back so I could get down. I wrote the ladder up as a safety hazard.

11
Interior Elements

Broken sash cords

The piece of wood on the window sill said "Window." When I opened the window, it was obvious that the intent was to use that stick to prop the window open, since the sash cords were no longer doing that job.

Older single- or double-hung windows used counterweights attached to sash cords to hold them in position. Without the cords and weights, a sash would simply fall back down when opened. This can be a serious safety issue, since a falling sash can lead to broken glass. Remember the end of the movie "Ghost"?

Older windows are costly to repair, and there are fewer and fewer companies equipped to do the work. Getting to the sash cord requires disassembling almost the entire window frame. Companies are much more inclined to sell you new windows instead. And, depending upon the window, it might actually be cheaper to replace the window than fix the old one. The oldest windows will use actual rope to connect the sash to the counterweight. Newer windows rely on springs. Whatever the mechanism, it is important that any windows that won't stay open by themselves be repaired. This is not just to prevent injury from broken glass or slamming on fingers, but also to make sure someone can get out through the window when needed. That's kind of hard to do when the window won't stay open to let you get out.

Failed seals

Dual pane windows are a great invention. They limit the amount of heat lost through the glass, and also help reduce noise transmission into the house. These windows have a gap between the panes, usually filled with an inert gas (usually nitrogen for lower-end windows; argon for higher-end ones).

As the windows age, it's pretty common for the sealant between the panes to deteriorate. This can allow air to get in between the panes, along with moisture. When the moisture evaporates, the minerals and dirt are left behind on the glass, where they build up to form a milky film that cannot be washed away. When we see a window like this, we report that it has a failed seal, and the sash should be replaced.

Why do we make a big deal about this? First of all, one of the primary functions of a window is to let in light and allow people inside to see out.

The intent is to be able to see clearly through a window. Failed seals allow minerals to build up between the panes and cloud the view. Sash replacement is the only permanent fix.

When the glass is cloudy, the window cannot perform either of these functions well.

With old single-pane windows, it was usually possible to replace just the glass in a sash. With double-pane windows, the sashes are manufactured as a unit in the factory, so it's not simply a matter of replacing the glass; the whole sash has to be replaced. Fortunately, this isn't a very complicated job, but if the windows are old, it could be difficult to get a good match for color, especially if the manufacturer is no longer producing that particular model.

Rot on windows

The organic materials used to build a house are not everlasting. Given enough time, even the best-built wooden structure will eventually succumb to the elements; water will get into the framing and rot the wood. The builder's job is to put everything together in such a way that the water stays out, and the homeowner's job is to maintain the exterior to keep that barrier working.

The only way to build a house that won't let any water in is to build it without any penetrations: No windows, doors, vents, skylights, chimneys. However, that's not practical! So anywhere there is a hole in the exterior, it needs to be constructed to shed water, and it needs upkeep to continue doing its job.

Windows that are poorly installed or not maintained will not be able to effectively keep water out, and will start to deteriorate. If the problem is not addressed, the water will eventually get into the framing and cause hidden damage. Repairing the problem will require removing the drywall from the entire affected area, replacing the rotted wood,[30] and restoring the finished surface. Not an inexpensive proposal!

There are two ways water can get into a window. The first is if it was not installed properly when the house was built. Typically, this means the flashing was done poorly, or omitted entirely. Older windows required flashing to be fabricated on site, with the joints properly overlapped. Then vinyl windows were introduced, which came as pre-assembled units,

---

30   *This is a structural repair, so it will require an engineer's input, with stamped drawings, and a building permit.*

complete with flashing, ready to be popped into a rough opening and nailed into place. Sure, vinyl windows themselves won't rot, but even these can be installed wrong, leading to damage inside the walls.[31]

Wood windows not only have to be installed correctly, but also require regular maintenance to keep the wooden elements from decaying. Here's an interesting twist: the older the window, the less maintenance it will likely need! This is because old wood (and by this I mean dating to the early 20th century or older) is more likely to be "old growth." This is very dense hardwood, such as oak or chestnut, that is slow-growing and has very tight growth rings. This density keeps water from soaking into the lumber once it's been cut, so it is more naturally rot-resistant. Some species like redwoods or old cedar that are both dense and have a lot of resin can even be termite-resistant.

Most modern lumber comes from fast-growing species such as pine or poplar, which has wider growth rings, making it soft enough for water to soak into the cut surfaces. Windows made with new lumber require regular painting or staining to keep them water resistant, otherwise they will deteriorate.

Dual key deadbolts

In an emergency, you want to be able to get out of the house as quickly as possible. In an ideal world, doors to the outside would be unlocked, opening immediately when the knob is turned. Unfortunately, exterior doors also have to serve as barriers to unauthorized entry, so they are typically locked, typically with a deadbolt that slides into the door frame.

Every residence is required to have one door that meets certain criteria to be the "primary egress." This must be a hinged door at least 32 inches wide, and it is not allowed to have a dual key deadbolt. In most houses, this is the front door[32].

Many doors have glass panels in them, or next to them, and homeowners may be concerned that someone will break the glass, reach in,

---

31   *I've seen everything from windows installed inside-out, sideways, and upside down, and even regular windows used as skylights.*

32   *Although these days the front door seems to be the least-used door in the house; for most people, the garage has become the primary entry and exit.*

Quick; where's the key? Dual-key deadbolt locks should not be used on exterior doors, and are not allowed at all on the primary egress door (typically the front door).

and turn the latch on the deadbolt. So they install a lock that requires a key on the inside as well. This is called a dual cylinder, or dual-key, deadbolt.

So what's the big deal? Just this: any time a door requires "special knowledge" to operate, it is unsafe. This knowledge could include locating the key, or how to bypass a child safety device, or anything else that may slow down a person's exit from the property during an emergency. Exterior doors, and especially the main entry door, should have a single-cylinder thumb-turn latch so the deadbolt can be unlocked quickly.

If a homeowner is concerned about security, I suggest they install plexiglass panels over the inside of any glass within reach of the door lock. This will likely thwart someone trying to break in as it will slow them down. Then I remind my client that my priority is to make sure the house is as safe as possible for the occupants. If someone really wants to break into your home, they will find a way, no matter what kind of locks you have. As a contractor once told me, "locks are made for honest people."

Loose Railings/Handrails

Before I start up a staircase, I always give the handrail a tug to see if it is loose. Same thing with guard rails. These things are put there to protect people from falls, and if they are loose, they cannot do their jobs properly, and someone could be hurt.

There are a lot of specifications that these components must meet: heights, widths, spacing, location, and more. These specifications can vary between jurisdictions, but the general rule is that any staircase with three or more risers must have a handrail, and any surface more than 30 inches high must have a guard rail.

Sometimes people want to get creative with their handrails.[33] They have a nautical theme going, so they use rope for a handrail. Or they have elaborate wrought iron scrollwork as a baluster. Both of these things defeat the main purpose of these items: to keep the occupants safe and protect them from falls.

Railings are supposed to prevent anyone from falling from an elevated surface. Any railing must be able to withstand a 200-pound force applied anywhere along its length without deflecting more than about half an inch. That's not a whole lot!

The worst offenders for loose railings are the short sections that project out from a wall at the top of a staircase. Being anchored only at one end means they are prone to loosening, and they are very difficult to tighten up.

There's so much wrong here! There's no proper lighting; the handrail is too short, it isn't secured to the wall and was very loose; and that second step down is much deeper than the rest.

---

33   *I blame Pinterest.*

If a person stumbles on a staircase, the handrail should be solid and secure enough for them to grip quickly and tightly to check their fall. A loose rope does not meet these criteria. The rise in popularity of home improvement shows and Pinterest has meant an increase in pretty, but unsafe, handrails and guardrails. This is a decorating trend you really don't want to "fall" for!

Excessive Air Fresheners

I've been in houses where every single room had an air freshener in it; some had multiple fresheners. The entire house would be cloaked in a haze of some vaguely floral scent. These often turn out to be houses with severe issues: either bad water intrusion and organic growths, or some other air quality problem like filthy ductwork or pet stains.

A properly maintained home, with good ventilation and an HVAC system in good working order, should have no issues with pervasive odors. Sometimes a house that has been vacant for an extended period will smell very musty when we first walk in the door; this kind of odor problem is difficult to treat with air fresheners as most fresheners rely on air movement to distribute the scent.

In an occupied home, lots of air fresheners could also mean that a smoker lives there. Again, this is a very difficult smell to eradicate, as cigarette smoke permeates the wall finishes and other surfaces and can stay there for years, affecting the indoor air quality.

If I see a lot of air fresheners in a house, I will look very carefully for signs of water problems and organic growths.

9" x 9" Floor Tiles

Asbestos has been used in buildings for centuries.[34] Its durability and fire-resistant properties made it useful for many applications, such as insulation and roofing materials. In the 1920s, it was used in a new resilient flooring tile, which was typically a dark color, 9 inches square. It was a wildly popular product, and during the post-war building boom accounted for more than a quarter of all residential flooring sales.

---

34 *More on asbestos in Chapter 20: Environmental Hazards.*

These tiles have the mottled and speckled coloring typical of asbestos-containing floor tiles. They are also the hallmark 9" square size.

Not only did the tiles contain asbestos, but the mastic used to adhere them did as well, and often had an even higher percentage. This makes removal a risky proposition, since there's a big risk of releasing asbestos fibers into the air when scraping this mastic off the floor.

As long as the tiles are not damaged, the health risk is minimal, since the asbestos is firmly embedded in the asphalt substrate. The issue come when the tiles are broken, or if they are subject to constant wear or abrasion from daily scrubbing or buffing. Any of these conditions can release fibers. The best thing to do for any asbestos flooring is to completely cover it up with another material that will protect it from wear and damage. This is called Encapsulation.

There are several ways to encapsulate a floor. The most common method is to simply lay another floor over it, preferably a sheet vinyl, making sure that all the tiles are completely protected.[35] As long as this new flooring stays intact, there is virtually no chance of exposure. For even more protection, the entire floor can be covered with a thin layer of concrete.

The biggest issue with these tiles is the perception of risk, and every potential buyer has a different risk tolerance. I've had clients who aren't concerned about asbestos tiles at all, especially if the floors are in good shape. They understand the chance of exposure is minimal. I've also had

---

35   *This may mean having to move appliances or HVAC equipment, since these were usually installed after flooring was already in place.*

clients walk away from houses like this, simply from hearing the "A" word. I will usually advise my client to have them completely encapsulated to eliminate as much risk as possible.

Pull-Down Attic Stairs

Pull-down stairs are pre-made assemblies that are sized for certain ceiling heights. The manufacturer will have very specific installation instructions regarding how to cut the legs to fit the space available. Legs that are too short will not provide proper support for someone climbing the stairs, and legs that are too long will not allow the stair segments to align properly, again posing a safety hazard. The only fix for stairs that are too short is to completely replace the entire stair assembly; there are no approved methods to repair a problem like this. For stairs that are too long, it may be possible to cut the legs to the correct length, as long as there has been no damage to the rest of the assembly.

The stairs we see on inspections usually do have the legs more or less of the correct length. But in far too many cases, we see the improper fastener used to attach the stairs to the attic framing. Using the wrong fastener can cause the stairs to collapse with someone on them; every year homeowners - and home inspectors! - are injured from collapsing stair assemblies. The usual culprit? Drywall screws.

Most attic stair manufacturers require that their stairs be installed with at least sixteen 16-penny nails driven into the framing. Nails have shear strength; that is, they are designed to withstand forces perpendicular to their

When all else fails, read the instructions. I wish this was a rare defect; unfortunately, it's not.

length. In contrast, drywall screws have very little shear strength; they are designed to withstand tension, or the force pulling them straight out along their length.

Luckily the fix for this is very simple: pound in the required nails in the required places and you should be good to go. But please: be mindful of the weight rating of the stairs! One person at a time.

Old Staircases

This is one of the things I have to call out as "the charm of the older home." Standards for staircases have been around for quite a while; the "Life Safety Code" of 1913 was an early effort to make sure houses, apartments, and commercial buildings were designed so that people could get out safely in the event of a fire. These rules included minimums and maximums for stairway width, tread depth, and riser height, along with numerous other requirements.

Prior to the rise of standard building codes, craftsmen simply built according to their own habits and experience. Stairways took up a lot of

One of the steepest staircases we've come across in an older home. There was about four feet of headroom. The easiest way to correct this would be to pull out the stairs and put in an elevator.

valuable space, so they were made as small as possible. Hence, lots of old houses have narrow, steep staircases that would never be allowed today. The issue here is that it is virtually impossible to correct an inherent defect like this; changing the configuration of a staircase involves wholesale alteration of floor framing, load paths, room layout, and a lot more issues. If the staircases are stacked, changing one will require changing them all.

Like I said, it's part of the "charm of the older home." People who live in houses with old staircases simply have to be aware of the hazards, and warn visitors to hold onto the handrails.

12
Electrical System

Service Drop Through Trees

My client was getting a "home checkup" inspection, just to find out what kinds of maintenance work and repairs she should be planning for. I arrived at the inspection site and started doing my usual exterior walk-around. When I got to the overhead electrical service wires, I saw they were going through the branches of a large tree in the front yard. One branch seemed to be resting on the wires themselves. But something else just looked wrong, although it took me a moment to spot it:

The neutral wire running between the power pole and the house had broken, meaning the house was only getting service from the two hot wires. This is a serious and immediate safety hazard, and was something I had never seen before. I asked the owner to call the power company and report the problem and to request an immediate repair.

The bucket truck showed up within ten minutes, and the service technician quickly spliced the neutral and got everything properly connected again. As he was finishing up, the homeowner asked me, "Could this be why we were having problems with our surge suppressors beeping all the time?"

Without that neutral line connecting the house and the power company lines, it's possible for the electrical service to become unbalanced, and with no neutral to carry the excess current, the house's wiring can become overloaded and cause a fire, or appliances can be damaged or destroyed. This particular house also had metal siding, and that siding could have become electrified as well. I actually did touch the siding before I noticed the broken wire, so I was extremely lucky in this case. Now I always look at the service entry before I even approach the house!

Service drop cables running through trees are prone to damage, as in the case above. Branches can abrade the cables and cause them to snap, or wear away the insulation and cause a fire. Any branches that can be blown into contact with wires should be trimmed back. Ideally, the tree itself should be removed to prevent any possibility of damage to the lines.

The insulation protecting this service entry cable is completely worn away, and the entire cable must be replaced as soon as possible. You should never see any wires on this cable; they can carry current, and can cause serious injury or lead to a fire.

Worn Service Entry Cable

There are two ways to get power to a home: underground and overhead. One of the advantages of underground wiring is the wires are protected from the elements, which keeps them from deteriorating. Overhead service has two components: the service drop, which reaches from the transformer to the splice, and the service entry (SE for short), which goes from the splice to the meter box.

It's important to understand who owns which segment of the wires, and who has responsibility for replacement. The power company owns the service drop wires, but the homeowner is responsible for keeping trees on their own property from coming into contact with them. The homeowner owns the SE cable from the splice onward. Also, the homeowner owns the meter enclosure, but the meter itself belongs to the power company.

Overhead service drops are constantly exposed to wind, rain, critters, trees, and sunlight, all of which can cause damage to the insulation around the wires. If the drop wires are damaged, the power company comes out and repairs or replaces them. But if the SE cable is worn or damaged, the homeowner needs to have it replaced at their expense.

When the outer jacket protecting the wires is worn away, you can see the silver wires wrapped around the core. Many people think these are ground wires, which typically don't carry any current, but this is actually the neutral, and it can sometimes be energized if there are wiring problems inside the house. If these wires are exposed, it is a shock and fire hazard, requiring replacement of the entire SE cable. This wire must be one continuous piece from the splice to the meter; it cannot be repaired by splicing in a new piece or wrapping it with tape.

No GFCIs

Every year, about 300 people are electrocuted in homes, and most of these deaths could have been prevented by installing a simple $20 device: the Ground Fault Circuit Interrupter (GFCI). This is a safety device based on the principle that water and electricity don't play well together, and we're mostly water, which is a great conductor.

Electricity needs a complete circuit to flow. If the switch is off, power won't flow and the wire should be "dead." But it isn't, really. Electricity is still flowing to the switch from the panel, and if you were to touch the bare conductor of the "hot" wire (usually the black or red one), you will get a nasty surprise. Switches work because the "off" position creates enough of a space between the wires of the circuit so that electricity won't jump the gap between them (creating an arc). This doesn't mean the electricity isn't still trying to complete its appointed rounds!

In a normal 110-volt circuit, power comes in via the "hot" wire and leaves via the "neutral" wire. If the neutral is not working properly, the excess power has to go somewhere, so it goes to the ground wire, which is typically a bare copper wire. However, water is a great conductor of electricity, so if the wiring is exposed to water, the electricity wants to flow through that too.

This water can either be in a bathtub, a flooded basement, or a puddle on the sidewalk. Any time wires come into contact with water, there's the potential for shock and electrocution. If the water happens to be contained in a person, the risk is the same.

GFCIs were first required in 1973 for exterior circuits near swimming pools. Bathrooms started requiring them in 1975, kitchens in 1987, and gradually more and more locations were added to the list. Now, any receptacle that is at all likely to come into contact with moisture is required to be GFCI protected.

Many older homes haven't been updated to provide full protection.[36] However, if there have been any renovations done, like an updated kitchen or bathroom, those areas must be brought up to the current codes. I see many houses with unprotected kitchen and bathroom circuits, and always recommend upgrading them to prevent injury or death from electrical shock.

Hazardous Electrical Panels

Do you know the brand of your electrical panel? Most people don't, and don't realize that it matters to the safety of the house and anyone doing work on the wiring.

---

36   *Remember, building codes are not retroactive.*

All three of these panels are considered hazardous and should be replaced. (Left) Federal Pacific Stab-Lok panels have a distinctive white rectangle between the breakers. (Center) Zinsco panels have wide color-coded breaker handles. (Right) Bulldog Pushmatic breakers have square center buttons.

There are three brands of panel that we always report as hazardous and recommend they be replaced as soon as possible: Federal Pacific, Zinsco, and Bulldog Pushmatic.

Federal Pacific Electric (FPE Stab-Lok) was a widely-distributed brand throughout the United States. These panels were supposed to be the future of electrical panels when they were introduced in the 1950s. They were widely used in millions of homes until the 1980s. But electricians and home inspectors soon started seeing problems with the panels; the breakers would fail to properly stop the flow of electricity when they tripped. This meant power would continue to flow through unsafe wires, leading to fires. Independent testing has shown that FPE breakers fail to trip as much as 70 to 80 percent of the time, a rate much higher than any other brand.

While there never was an "official" recall of these panels, there was a class action suit, and a New Jersey State Court ruled that the Federal Pacific Electric (FPE) Company "violated the Consumer Fraud Act because FPE knowingly and purposefully distributed circuit breakers which were not tested to meet UL standards..."[37]

---

37   *Superior Court of New Jersey, Middlesex County Division; Docket No. L-2904-97*

With Bulldog Pushmatic panels, the issue is also the breakers. Like the FPE breakers, Pushmatic breakers had a history of failure to properly shut off power. But there was a special issue with the Pushmatic breakers: in order to keep them in working condition, they required regular maintenance, which included exercising the breakers (that is, turning them off and on again) on a regular basis, and also lubricating the breakers. Not many homeowners were made aware of these requirements, and regular maintenance of the breakers was usually not done. As a result, the breaker mechanisms were made even more susceptible to failure.

Not only that, the trip indicator flag on a breaker would get stuck in either the on or off position, giving a false indication of its state. So even if the circuit was live, the indicator may show it as off, and this is a significant shock hazard.

With Zinsco panels, the problem lies with the connection between the breaker and the bus bar, which is the part of the panel that carries the electricity from the service wire. Breakers clip onto this bar to transfer the electricity to the wires.

Zinsco breakers often failed to make a good connection to the bus bar. As a result, they had a tendency to cause arcing, which led to fires. The arcing could also fuse the breaker to the bus bar, preventing its removal. Or, the connection could become so loose that if the deadfront panel were removed, all the breakers would simply fall out.

It's what you can't see in bad panels that should concern you. These burn marks are from breakers arcing on the bus bars. This could lead to a devastating house fire.

The company was purchased by Sylvania, which produced panels for several years under the Zinsco-Sylvania label. Finally, the design was discontinued.

With all three of these brands, we hear from homeowners that "It's been there for 30 years and hasn't caused a problem." That may be so, but there is simply no way to know whether the breakers will react when needed. The failure rate of these brands means you cannot rely on them to protect your home from a potentially catastrophic fire.

Some electricians don't see a problem with these panels; their main issue is that breakers are no longer readily available, so adding circuits is difficult. We always tell our clients that these panels should be replaced with a modern panel. If the electrician disagrees, ask them to state their professional opinion in writing, on official company letterhead, along with their license number and assertion that the panels do not present a risk. It's amazing how many times they will suddenly decide that replacement is prudent after all.

Painted Receptacles

I get it; electric plugs are ugly. They're white or ivory, don't match the walls, and if the room is a dark color they stand out like sore thumbs. This doesn't mean that you can cover them with paint, yet I see it all the time.

This receptacle was so clogged with paint that I couldn't insert my tester into either position. This can't be cleaned; it will have to be replaced.

There are several issues with painted electrical receptacles. First of all, if the paint is thick enough, it's impossible to actually plug anything into them! I've seen receptacles that are so clogged with paint all the holes are completely covered over.

If you force a plug into a painted receptacle, it's possible that some of the paint will chip off and be shoved inside. These chips can then act as conductors, allowing electricity to flow inside the receptacle, and potentially causing arcing. This is a major hazard that can lead to smoldering fires inside the walls.

Paint on the surface of the receptacle can act as a conductor as well, letting electricity flow across the prongs if they are not fully seated. This can cause not only arcing and fires, but is a serious shock hazard to the person using the plug!

I always mark these receptacles as requiring replacement. Go ahead and paint or wallpaper the outside of the cover plate, but please don't decorate the receptacle itself.

Knob and Tube Wiring

One of the earliest standardized methods of distributing electricity throughout a house was knob and tube wiring. It was most commonly used between about 1880 and 1930, and is readily identified by the porcelain insulators that allow the wires to change direction (the knobs) and pass through wooden framing (the tubes).

While it worked as a system, there were limitations. It had to be exposed to air, since the wires tended to heat up during use, so any framing cavities with the wires in them could not be insulated. As you can imagine, this meant that houses were pretty energy-inefficient. That may not have been an issue back when oil and gas were relatively inexpensive, but in today's economy, an uninsulated house will be a complete energy hog, with astronomical heating and cooling bills.

Many mortgage companies will not underwrite loans on homes with active knob and tube wiring, due to the increased risks. Likewise, insurance companies will probably not issue a homeowners policy on the property.

Typical knob and tube wiring. This can often be spotted in attics or unfinished basements. Be careful if you see it; it could very well be live.

Knob and tube systems are also not grounded, since they are two wire systems (hot and neutral). This increases the potential for shock injuries, especially when homeowners use adapters that let them plug a three-prong plug into a two-wire receptacle.

Correcting this problem requires rewiring the entire house to meet modern standards. This includes running all new wiring and probably replacing the main electrical panel as well, if it has fuses rather than breakers. But this is only part of the cost: getting to all the wiring will likely require removing a lot of finished wall area[38] to get at it, plus the wiring must be accessible for permit inspections.

Just because you see the knobs and tubes and wires in a house doesn't mean there's a problem, though. Sometimes, homeowners like to leave them in place as part of the "charm" of the older home when they have new wiring installed. A non-contact voltage tester will reveal whether the wires are live, and until I've tested them, I always assume they are.

One of the concerns with replacing knob and tube is, "did they get it all?" There really is no way to say definitively that every bit of old wiring was removed unless you open up every wall to check. An electrician can do an extensive forensic examination of all the wiring and can probably tell if there is anything left, but it's beyond the scope of a home inspection.

---

38   *Which is probably plaster and lath if the house is old enough. Repairing plaster walls can be double the cost of drywall.*

Aluminum Wiring

Copper has been the preferred material for electrical wiring for decades. Its flexibility and electrical conductivity make it the most practical choice.

During the Vietnam War (roughly 1965-1972), copper became scarce and expensive; it was needed for ammunition. But the post-WWII building boom was still in full swing, and an alternative material was needed to wire all the houses. Enter Aluminum: flexible, with good conductivity, and more readily available.

Unfortunately, aluminum wiring has a problem. It expands and contracts more than copper does when it gets hot. This means that electrical connections tend to loosen over time due to the cyclical heating and cooling of the wires. Loose connections mean arcing, which can lead to fires.

Spotting aluminum wiring is difficult without opening up the electrical panel or pulling out a receptacle. Some houses with aluminum wiring may have had the connections "pig-tailed" with COPALUM crimps, which is one of the few approved methods for correcting the problem.

It is important to know that the only approved methods of pig-tailing aluminum wiring are COPALUM connectors, which must be installed with a highly specialized tool, or AlumiConn(TM) aluminum wiring repair connectors. We have seen pigtailing done with simple blue wire nuts; this is no longer an approved method and can cause fires due to improper connections.

The two wires on the bottom breaker are solid aluminum conductors. This type of wiring may cause arcing and fire and needs to be repaired or replaced.

Rust this bad is visible without even taking the front cover off. The entire panel and all the breakers will need to be replaced.

The other issue with aluminum wiring, one that is not solved by pig-tailing, is that it can become brittle over time, especially if it is subject to movement. The wires can develop cracks, which can lead to arcing and fires. In this case, the only remedy is to remove all the aluminum wiring and replace it with copper.

Some aluminum wire is still used, but only multi-stranded varieties. These don't have the same issues as the single-strand aluminum branch wiring, and are usually used for high-capacity appliances like dryers and ranges. Aluminum is even used for the service entry cables that bring power from the street to your house. Even so, some jurisdictions are banning the use of aluminum wires for interior circuits.

If your house has aluminum wiring and you do not address it either by rewiring or pig-tailing, you must be vigilant about spotting potential problems. Flickering lights and "popping" light switches are signs that there are issues inside the walls; the affected circuits should be turned off at the breaker and an electrician called to make repairs.

Water/Rust in Panel

As I said in the section on GFCIs, water and electricity don't play well together. If I look at an electrical panel and see rust, I know that water has gotten into it or onto it at some point in the past.

Rust is a sign of damaged metal, and could mean that the electrical connections inside the panel or the breakers themselves are no longer secure. Rust can lead to arcing, which leads to fire or electric shock.

So how does water get into a panel anyway? A lot of the time, it travels along the outside of the service entry cable, especially if the entry point on the outside wall isn't sealed properly. Or, water could be getting into the basement due to poor drainage or grading, and it just happens to be where the panel is.

It doesn't take a leak to cause rust, though. I inspected a house built in the 1890s, where the electrical panel was located in an unfinished cellar with a dirt floor. The humidity level was extremely high, which meant that moisture would condense on any cool surface, and anything metal is a prime target. The box was almost all rust, and would need to be replaced.

There's a rule of thumb about contaminants in electrical panels: if the material cannot be removed with a dry cloth (no cleansers or solvents), the panel must be replaced.[39] Not only that, but all the breakers will need to be replaced as well, since their internal components may also be rusty and there's no way to open them to check; once they've been cracked open, they have to be replaced.

Inadequate Work Area

It was a cute little house, with a lot of charm and a "recently remodeled" kitchen. Those two words often set off alarm bells for home inspectors. While most remodeling jobs are done beautifully, some can conceal major issues.

I did my usual walk through the house, mentally noting the locations of all the major systems. But I didn't find the electrical panel. I figured I would come across it eventually.

The kitchen was gorgeous, with granite countertops and beautiful wood cabinets with integrated lights and leaded glass doors. A room next to the kitchen had been converted into a butler's pantry, with built-in display shelving and matching cabinetry and counters. I opened a base cabinet door

---

39   *Rust is the primary contaminant we see, followed closely by paint overspray.*

(Left) Why is there a loose side panel in the base cabinet? (Right) How else were you going to access the electrical panel? This was written up as a major safety hazard.

by the wall and noticed something... odd. The cabinet panel facing the wall appeared to be removable. I moved the panel and saw... the electrical panel.

This panel failed all sorts of safety rules. Electrical panels are supposed to have a minimum safe working area of 30" wide and 36" deep, and tall enough to allow a person to stand at the panel to service it. This panel couldn't be opened safely by anyone. My client asked if the fix would be expensive. "Well," I told her, "The base and wall cabinets on this wall will need to be removed to access the panel. They would then have to be redesigned to allow adequate access to the panel. Or, the panel can be moved to another location, but that will still involve taking the cabinets out to get at the panel. Then there will be the expense of putting in a new panel and rewiring all the circuits to it."

My client did elect to cancel the contract for the house, and I was left to wonder how any self-respecting contractor would allow the panel to be obstructed like that.

Most of the time, poor access is just a matter of moving furniture or belongings out of the way. But sometimes, we will run across a situation where a homeowner has constructed a barrier that makes removing the panel cover too dangerous for an inspector to do safely. Removing deadfronts is the second most dangerous part of the inspection (walking

This is not the correct way to make a connection for an attic vent fan. The box and wiring are not supported, the wires are exposed to the box's sharp edges, and the wire junctions are just taped. The good news is that correcting this is not a huge job... but it makes me wonder what other electrical defects are present.

roofs is first), and unless I feel I have enough room to maneuver the cover off safely, I'm going to call for an electrician to render a verdict on its location.

Visible Wirenuts

What happens when two pieces of electrical wire need to be connected? It's not like a string of Christmas lights, where you just have to plug them together. Instead, the insulation is stripped from the ends, and they are twisted together with a wire nut. This plastic device has a metal coil inside that grabs the wires and holds them securely to allow a good connection between them. The goal is to make the connection as solid as possible, so that the flow of electricity is not impeded, and there is minimal risk of arcing.

Any connection between two pieces of wire is called a junction, and any junctions must be enclosed within a junction box. These metal boxes protect the wires and junctions from anything that might cause the connections to weaken: water, vibration, critters,[40] and the like. Also, since any wire connection has the potential to arc, the boxes are fireproof, and can prevent a fire by keeping any arcing confined to the box itself.

All too often, we see defective wire junctions: no wire nuts, or not contained within a junction box. These are all written up as fire hazards.

---

40   *Did you know mice like to gnaw on live electrical wires? Yeah, we see a lot of mouse carcasses near chewed-up wires.*

Not only that, but keep in mind that we can only report on what we see; there could be more dangerous connections concealed behind the walls. The only way to know for sure is to open up the walls and visually confirm that every junction is properly made and properly connected. This is why permits are so important! Any time new wires are run, permits should be pulled and the proper inspections done by the local authorities. This way, any potential issues can be spotted before they are covered up.

Another rule about wire junctions is that they must all be accessible. This means that you cannot make a wire junction, even within a junction box, and then cover it up with drywall. The junction box should have a solid metal cover plate on it that can be removed to inspect the wires. So if you see a blank wall plate, there is probably a junction box behind it.

Burns/Scorch Marks

When two wires are not connected properly, there is the potential for arcing. This is when electricity literally jumps the gap between the wires, flowing through the air instead of through the copper. But air has more resistance than copper, and if you remember your high school physics, electrical resistance creates heat.[41] So the wires get hot, which affects the flow of electricity, which builds up more heat, and eventually the insulation around the wire starts to smoke and melt. If the condition isn't corrected,

Both outlets on this receptacle are scorched; there are likely some serious electrical issues with this circuit, and maybe more as well that just haven't acted up... yet.

---

41   *And light. This is literally why incandescent light bulbs work, and why they get so hot.*

it can result in a fire that can spread inside the walls and throughout the house.

Scorch marks in and around electrical components are a sign that there is a poor wire connection nearby. If the marks are on a receptacle, it could mean that the receptacle isn't making a good connections with the prongs of a plug. Any such receptacle needs to be replaced.

Even more concerning are scorch marks inside the main breaker panel. This can point to multiple problems, including undersized wires, oversized breakers, loose connections, contaminants, and more.

Any wire that has been heated to the point where the insulation is affected needs to be replaced, since this kind of stress reduces the wire's ability to conduct electricity. This is called "derating" and can lead to an increased risk of fire. If the damage is bad enough, an electrician may decertify the entire panel, requiring complete replacement of the panel and all the breakers.

Undersized Service

Sometimes the problem with the electrical service is simply that it is old. Older homes with gas appliances (furnace, water heater and stove) could get by with electrical service as low as 50-65 amps, but this is simply inadequate for today's lifestyles. They didn't have to worry about high-energy use appliances like air conditioners or clothes dryers, microwaves, toasters, coffee makers, hair dryers, etc. Homes built prior to about 1920 may also have knob and tube wiring, as well as old-style fuse boxes. All of these present fire hazards and will require complete electrical overhauls. Rewiring an old home to bring it up to date electrically can be very expensive, especially if wiring needs to be replaced inside the walls.

Power companies are happy to sell you as much power as you want, and will sometimes install the new service lines from the street at little or no cost to the home owner. This is called a heavy-up. If I inspect a house that has under 100 amps of power or less, I will usually recommend getting a heavy-up, simply to allow the occupants to use all the various power-using appliances they are accustomed to. In general, the smallest service that is practical in today's world is 150 amps An all-electric home needs at least 200 amps. Big houses often have 400 amps, split between two panels..

Notes from the Field

One of the challenges of the home inspection process is trying to explain issues in such a way that the client really understands the problem. I usually ask clients what their day jobs are, or what their profession is, because it can help me use analogies to frame issues more clearly.

One of my favorite analogies is cars. Everyone understands cars and can relate to the things that happen to them. For example, when I talk about a roof that has a serviceable life of 17 years, I compare that to 40,000-mile tires. How many miles you get on those tires will depend a lot on your driving style: jackrabbit starts will shave years off the tread, while a cautious driver who sticks to smooth roads and the speed limit could get more than the expected use from those same tires. Same thing with roofs. If you take care of your roof, keep trees away from it, clear any debris promptly, and stay on top of any minor repairs, that 17-year roof could last much longer.

Another analogy is furnace and air conditioner efficiency. Think about old cars: they get lousy mileage and don't have the features that new cars do. That old clunker may still get you to your destination, but a newer car will be more efficient and you will probably have no issues with finding parts for it.

This Tiny House has all the comforts of home, plus mobility. It was on display at InspectionWorld 2018 in Orlando.

See the details at www.hummingbirdhousing.com

13
Plumbing System

Galvanized Pipes

Galvanized iron pipes were in wide use until the 1950s for interior water supply and drainage, as well as for hydronic heating systems. The material has a serviceable life of about 50 years, so any of it still in use is considered to be past its serviceable life.

The problem with this pipe is that it corrodes along the inside, with rust deposits that build up on the walls like cholesterol in an artery. This reduces the flow, and the rust also eats away at the walls themselves, so they will eventually burst. These pipes often look just fine on the outside; once the damage is visible on the surface of the pipe, the wall of the pipe could be tissue-thin and ready to burst. Galvanized pipes should be replaced with modern materials (copper, CPVC, or PEX). This is a complicated and expensive fix, as it will require cutting holes in the walls and ceilings to

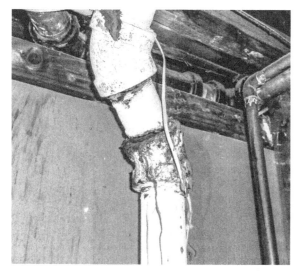

These waste pipes are completely eaten through. There are probably more like them in other places throughout the house, concealed inside the walls.

locate and get access to all the supply pipes, and then patching and restoring the finished surfaces.

There are companies that specialize in high-tech pipe repair that claim to be able to "re-line" old pipes with epoxy, which can be done without opening up walls and causing a mess. If you're faced with the prospect of having to redo your home's plumbing, one of these companies might be an alternative to a complete re-pipe.

Low or High Water Pressure

Water typically enters a house at the lowest level. Since water only flows downhill, it needs to be pushed to get to the upper floors. With private water wells, this is done with a pressurized tank; with municipal water, the pressure comes from the supply lines.

Water pressure inside a house should be somewhere between 30 and 80 pounds per square inch (PSI). This will push the water enough to get it to the upper level of a home without pushing it so hard that it will damage the pipes or fixtures. If the pressure is too low, upstairs bathrooms won't get adequate service. If it's too high, the force of the water can cause pipes to burst or fixtures to leak.

It's rare to have high pressure in a well system; more often it's a low pressure problem and it's from a waterlogged tank. Pressure problems in a municipal system can have a variety of causes.

High pressure is a delivery issue; the city is pumping the water too hard. The only way to fix this is to have a pressure regulator installed at the water line. If I see a regulator already installed and the house still has high water pressure, the regulator needs to be adjusted, repaired, or replaced.

Low pressure can be a delivery issue. A house at the very end of a city supply system may get so little pressure that a booster pump must be added to allow for adequate water flow. It can also be a problem with the piping; a leak in the main line between the city pipe and the house can cause a pressure drop inside. There can also be problems with the piping inside the house, especially if the interior pipes are galvanized (see previous section). These pipes can have corrosion built up inside them, like cholesterol blocking an artery, narrowing them and blocking the flow.

Not every low water pressure problem is systemic. If only a single faucet dribbles when you turn it on, it could simply mean a clogged aerator, or a partially closed valve. These are quick fixes.

Polybutylene Pipes

When we walked into the basement of this million-dollar-plus house, we were awed by the incredible assortment of Japanese artwork. There was a formal tea ceremony room, a meditation room, and a sitting room. Each was beautifully crafted with wooden floors, cabinetry, and more. Another

This connection between the copper water line on the left and the Polybutylene pipe on the right was on the verge of failure and threatened a basement full of priceless antiques.

This installation is a double whammy: polybutylene piping to all the fixtures in the home, coupled with "Big Blue" polybutylene supply pipe coming from the street. Polybutylene for outside use is typically "smurf blue" color, while interior pipe is gray.

part of the basement had a billiards room and bar, all done in gorgeous wood.

Bob and I were doing the inspection as a team, due to the size of the property (more than 11,000 square feet). The sellers were present, and were impatient for us to be finished as they were planning on going out of town for a three-day weekend as soon as we were done.

This house had been extensively remodeled: an addition with a full basement was connected to the original house via a crawl space. Bob managed to squeeze into the small opening and access the crawl while I started inspecting the kitchen. Within a few minutes, Bob came into the kitchen and addressed the owners.

"You need to call a plumber, right now," he told them. "You've got a section of Polybutylene piping that has a corroding connection, and it appears to be leaking."

"Okay," the owner said. "We'll call them when we get back into town."

"No, you need to call them now," Bob insisted. "This is a serious problem."

The owner begrudgingly called their plumber, who arrived about half an hour later. He went into the crawl space while we continued our inspection in the rest of the house.

Within seconds, we heard a panicked shout: "Shut it off!! Shut it all off!! Shut off the water!!!" Bob darted down to the basement and shut the water off, then located the plumber and asked what had happened. It turned out that he had simply touched the corroded junction piece, and it fell apart in his hands. Water immediately started gushing from the disconnected pipe. Fortunately, he was there to crimp the pipe with his hands until the water could be shut off, and no serious damage was done. The seller was grateful for our insistence; had the pipe burst while they were away, the entire basement would have been flooded - and all that artwork ruined.

Polybutylene (PB) piping was hailed as the "modern replacement for copper pipes" when it was introduced in the early 1980s. It was flexible, easy to install, and plumbers loved it. But then came the problems. It was vulnerable to deterioration from chlorinated city water. There were many cases of catastrophic damage due to burst fittings. A class action suit was brought against the manufacturer, and millions of dollars were paid out to settle claims for repairs and replacement. Many sellers tend to brush off the imminent danger; "It's been fine for 25 years. Nothing wrong with it!" But problems with PB can take a long time to develop. It all depends upon the quality of the fittings, and the chlorine level in the water.

We always recommend replacing all PB piping in a house. This is a major undertaking, and the cost usually starts at around $10,000.

ABS Glued to PVC

Plastic is the preferred material for interior drain pipes. It's inexpensive, easy to work with, and the joints can simply be glued rather than requiring precise cuts and threaded connectors, and it doesn't need soldering. Its main issue is that it is vulnerable to deterioration when exposed to ultraviolet radiation in sunlight; this makes it brittle and could cause it to shatter. Luckily, most of the time these pipes are located inside the walls.

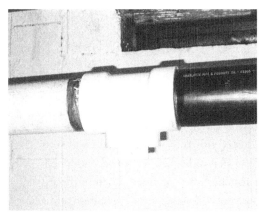

The white PVC pipe and connector on the left should not be glued to the black ABS pipe on the right; this joint will eventually leak.

The trouble with plastic piping is that there really isn't just one type of plastic. Homes can have many kinds: Polyvinyl chloride (PVC), Chlorinated PVC (CPVC), and Acrylonitrile butadiene styrene (ABS) are the most common, but newer homes will often have Crosslinked polyethylene (PEX) as well.

CPVC and PEX are meant for water supply pipes, while PVC and ABS are for drainage. It's not unusual to see a house with all four materials in the plumbing system, and there's nothing wrong with doing it that way… as long as the connections are done right.

Most plastic water pipe leaks happen at the joints, and are typically due to poor installation. The biggest problem comes when two different plastics are joined together. One of the big advantages of plastic is that it can be glued, but only if the two pieces being glued are the same type, and the glue used is the proper one for that type. Glue for plastic piping works by dissolving the surface of the pipes; as the glue cures, the two surfaces blend together and solidify, creating a secure and permanent bond. This is called "solvent welding." Each type of plastic requires its own adhesive to make a secure connection.

Any time I see a black plastic pipe and a white plastic pipe connected with a glued joint, I call it out as a potential leak risk. To properly transition between these two materials, they must be connected with a mechanical joint called a Fernco (TM). This is a rubber sleeve that is secured to both pipe ends with clamps. Any glued joint between ABS and PVC needs to be cut out and replaced with mechanical joints; fortunately, because these pipes aren't usually full of water (and it's not just water), this is a relatively simple fix... assuming the pipe is visible and accessible. Lots of plumbing drain pipes are concealed behind drywall, and if I spot one improper joint, there is the potential for more where I cannot see them.

Sump or Grinder Pump Blocked

There was an odd piece of pipe sticking out from the wall in the back yard, going into a section of flexible downspout extension. When I got inside, I saw the pipe come in through the wall and go downwards, disappearing behind a built-in bookcase over a brick kneewall. The owner happened to be present, so I asked him whether there was a sump pump behind there somewhere.

"Yes," he said. "It's under the bookcase, behind the brick wall." The bookcase was stuffed with the owner's record collection, which is why I hadn't been able to see that the whole section was removable. He cleared the shelves and moved the unit, and there was the sump pump.

It worked when I tested it, but the entire enclosure it sat in was damp and musty, and there were organic growths on the walls. There was no air circulation in that area at all, so any moisture that got in simply stayed there, making it a very hospitable environment for the growths.

(Left) I wonder what that white pipe is running along the wall behind the bookcase? (Center) The homeowner removed the bookcase for me. (Right) The concealed sump pump in a damp and musty enclosure.

A sump pump should be completely visible and accessible for maintenance and repair due to its critical role in keeping the basement dry. If you have no idea the pump isn't working right and the water isn't being drained properly, you won't know to fix it until the flooding reaches past whatever is blocking your view. By that time what could have been a very simple and inexpensive fix has turned into a costly restoration job.

Anything Wet

Water supply and drain pipes should keep their contents under control. There shouldn't be any water dripping from them. Not all water on the outside of a pipe is a leak, however. High humidity can cause condensation on the surface of a metal pipe, which can lead to corrosion from the outside inward, and could create holes in the pipe to let the water inside leak out.

When I'm going through a house, I'm always looking for signs that there is a pipe in distress somewhere. The clues are sometimes obvious: puddles on the floor means something is wrong, and I will look carefully at what is above the wet spot to see if the source is immediately visible.

Sometimes, though, there may not be a wet spot. There may not even be a leak! The only evidence of problems is rust or corrosion caused by condensation on pipes or ducts, and tracking down the source can take some detective work.

Sometimes it's fairly obvious that there is a leak.

The thing to remember is that water only flows downhill. So I follow the corrosion or rust upwards until I see where it stops; that's where I start looking for the problem. It usually turns out to be condensation on a metal duct or cold water line, but I've also found pretty severe corrosion caused by a humidifier that was installed in the ductwork by the furnace.

Things might also look wet that aren't; old cast iron plumbing soil stack pipes can have shiny patches on them that are usually leftovers from the old ways of connecting the sections with oakum, a tar-like substance that was originally used to seal planks on a ship's wooden hull.

People tend to forget about things like pipes until they break. Being aware of small warning signs like corrosion or tiny drips on the floor can help you nip the problem in the bud before you end up with a flooded house.

Gas Smell

Natural gas and liquid propane are low odor by themselves. This would be a safety hazard because leaks could go undetected and lead to explosions. Gas suppliers add a pungent odorant to the gas that is extremely obvious, just to make it very easy to detect even a very small leak.

You should never smell gas inside a house. You may get a small whiff of gas if you're turning on a burner of a gas stove, but that should go away

Gas meters have clearance requirements, and this one violates just about all of them. It should be 3 feet from the electrical disconnect, the air conditioner compressor, and the vent openings, and two feet from the hose bib.

almost immediately. If you step inside the front door and smell it, there is a real problem that could result in disaster. You should not do anything that might generate a spark: don't turn any lights on or off, don't operate anything electronic, and don't touch any metal surfaces. Get any people and pets outside and call 911 once you are clear of the house.

Gas explosions are extremely violent and can often damage or destroy surrounding properties, so alert the neighbors as well. The fire department will almost certainly cordon off the area until the gas is turned off and the inside completely aired out. You will then need to bring in a plumber[42] to locate the leak and repair it. The gas company will ask for proof of repair before restoring service to the house.

Because of the risk, I advise my clients to have any work involving gas lines or gas appliances done by professionals. In 2011, a home in Rockville, MD was leveled by a gas explosion after the occupants attempted to remove a gas dryer themselves and replace it with an electric one.

Charring on the joists and subfloor indicates there likely was a fire at this meter in the past. The homeowner is extremely fortunate they did not lose the entire house. Even so, the damaged framing needs to be repaired and reinforced, since charred wood is both weaker and more vulnerable to reignition.

---

42   *Why a plumber? Because most of them are also gasfitters.*

Notes from the Field

Part of the fun of teaching Home Inspection classes at Frederick Community College is running into former students who are happily engaged in their new careers. They come up and tell me about the interesting houses they're seeing, and how much they are enjoying the work that they do.

It's so satisfying knowing that I'm teaching the next generation of home inspectors. Some people ask me if I'm aware that I'm teaching my future competition. My response is always that these future home inspectors will be colleagues, not competition, and I want to make sure that they will represent the profession with skill and knowledge.

Devin was inspecting the house across the street and popped over to say hi when he saw my van!

Rose found me at a trade show and was so excited to tell me about her new career!

14
Heating, Ventilation, and Air Conditioning (HVAC)

Cracked Heat Exchanger

A furnace works by burning fuel, which creates hot exhaust. This exhaust is dangerous to breathe, so it can't just be circulated through the house. Instead, it passes through a series of channels, which pick up the heat. The house air passes over the other side of the channels and is warmed, and then gets distributed via the ducts. This channel assembly is called the heat exchanger.

Over the years, there have been technical advances in heat exchangers, and they have gotten better and better at extracting as much heat from the furnace exhaust as possible. In today's high-efficiency condensing gas furnaces, the exhaust is cool enough that it can be vented with plastic pipes instead of metal.

The exhaust air should never come into contact with the distribution air, so the heat exchanger must be free of any holes or gaps. The trouble is, the heat exchanger is hidden inside the furnace and has lots of bends and turns to increase the surface area, so spotting a small hole is extremely difficult. Most of the time, it's only found when carbon monoxide detectors start sounding.[43]

When I inspect a gas furnace, I look carefully at the flame pattern from the burners. It should be steady, without a lot of flickering and movement. If the flames jump around a lot, it's a sign that there is too much air movement going on, which could signal a crack or hole in the heat exchanger. It's not possible to repair a heat exchanger; once it is compromised, the entire furnace must be replaced.

How do heat exchangers get damaged in the first place? There are two main culprits: manufacturing defects, and corrosion.

A heat exchanger can fail due to bad welds, a flaw in the material itself, or faulty installation. In condensing gas furnaces, the condensate is also corrosive, so issues with the drainage can affect the heat exchanger too. Most furnaces also have air conditioning systems installed over them, and if the condensate from the air conditioner overflows the drain pan, it can drip onto the heat exchanger and cause corrosion.

Furnaces should be serviced annually; the technician will open up the cabinet and visually inspect all the interior components. They also have specialized tools to measure the air flow through and around the heat exchanger, which will identify problems in the system.

Under-Slab Ductwork

Not every house has a basement or even a crawl space; it can also be a "slab on grade," where the bottom floor rests directly on the ground. In many cases, utilities are embedded in this concrete slab during construction

---

43   *Another reason why we're so picky about having the proper safety equipment in a home. Before the advent of CO alarms, there were an awful lot of cases of "he died peacefully in his sleep."*

This under-slab duct shows water staining and some debris. You can also see the fibrous material in the duct; this is likely Transite, which is known to contain asbestos. Remediation will be expensive, as it usually requires replacing all the ductwork.

to avoid having to take up space inside the living area. One of the common elements in this type of layout is ductwork for heating and cooling.

If I am inspecting a house that is slab on grade and I see duct registers in the floor, I will remove the register covers and take a careful look inside the ducts. I'm looking for two specific things: organic growth, and Transite.

Under-slab ducts are notorious for harboring organic growths. Any moisture that seeps into the foundation can end up inside the duct, where it's virtually impossible to see. Any growths are then bathed in the air passing through the duct, and end up getting distributed throughout the house.

Here's the thing: these ducts were often made of Transite, which is known to contain asbestos. Disturbing the Transite can release asbestos fibers, so these under-slab ducts can't simply be cleaned the way metal ductwork can. The only real solution is to abandon the ductwork. This means permanently sealing up all the registers, and installing new ductwork inside the walls. As you can imagine, this is an expensive, messy proposition, and will probably involve having to take space from rooms for the ductwork to run through.

Inadequate Combustion Air

To burn any kind of fuel, you need air. Gas or oil furnaces need to have a steady supply of air to operate efficiently. If there's not enough combustion air, the result can be incomplete combustion or backdrafting, both of which can increase the level of carbon monoxide in the house.

Gas furnaces, especially older ones, are big and noisy. They take up floor space that homeowners would rather use for other purposes, so it's tempting to put them in as small a space as possible, and keep the door shut. But doing this can mean the furnace doesn't get enough air. Couple this with the fact that there's probably a gas water heater sharing the space with the furnace, and you've now got two gas appliances that are competing for the available air.

My clients are surprised when I tell them that appliances relying on room air for combustion need up to 50 cubic feet per 1,000 BTUs. So a 66,000 BTU furnace, which is a pretty common size, needs to be in a room that is about 20 feet by 21 feet, assuming it's an 8 foot ceiling. Add a gas water heater and you need an even larger space. If the room is smaller than that, the fuel cannot burn completely, which creates more toxic gases that can be released into the air.

This is one reason why fuel-burning appliances that rely on room air are not allowed in bedroom closets; the risk of carbon monoxide poisoning can be very real if the proper conditions aren't met. Fortunately, this problem goes away when you upgrade to a high-efficiency condensing furnace, which draws its combustion air directly from the outside, virtually eliminating the danger of inadequate air.

How do you know whether your furnace is high-efficiency? Just look at the vent pipe. If it's metal and goes up a chimney or flue, it is still drawing its air from the inside of the house. If there are two plastic pipes that go straight from the furnace and out the wall to the outside of the house, it's a condensing furnace.

Backdrafting

Exhaust from a fuel-burning appliance should only go in one direction: up and out. Exhaust gases are health hazards, as they contain carbon monoxide (CO). This gas is colorless and odorless, and is dangerous because it binds to blood cells, preventing them from taking up oxygen. With enough CO exposure, a person will suffocate. Every year, an average of 430 people die from CO poisoning.

There are a lot of ways exhaust gases can make their way out of a flue and into the home. There can be holes in a flue, or sections could become separated. But even an intact flue can be subject to another avenue: backdrafting.

Air is constantly entering and leaving a house. Windows are opened, bathroom fans are turned on, dryers vent outside. Air that leaves puts the house under negative pressure, and nature will try to balance the pressure by bringing air in from another opening. In older homes, this usually wasn't a problem; there were lots of gaps around windows and in the walls where air could get in.[44] Backdrafting wasn't as big an issue then, since fresh air was coming in through these gaps. But as houses started getting more airtight and energy-efficient, the incidence of CO poisoning went up as well.

Nature does not like imbalances, and when you pull air out of a house you are lowering the air pressure inside. This is called "negative pressure," and it just means that the air pressure inside something is lower than it is outside something. The higher pressure is then drawn towards the lower

The staining, rust and debris visible on the draft hood of this old furnace could be indications of poor drafting, which can allow exhaust fumes to enter the house.

---

44   *This is why old houses are called "drafty."*

pressure to balance things out. So if you are pulling air out, air needs to come back in from some other source. It will come in through the path of least resistance, and a flue is just a big open pipe to the outside. If enough air is being sucked out, air trying to get inside to balance the pressure will reverse the flow of any exhaust gases and send them back into the house. This is called backdrafting, and it's a life-threatening defect.

The most common appliance for backdrafting is a natural-draft water heater. These have weaker drafts than furnaces, so take less negative pressure to reverse the flow. Backdrafting leaves telltale marks at the base of the flue: melted plastic on the water line gaskets, corrosion and stains on the top of the heater, and dark streaks going outward from the flue. If any of these signs are present, the water heater and the entire HVAC system need to be evaluated for proper drafting.

Sometimes the problem comes from interior fans that are too strong. Kitchen range hoods that pull more than 400 cubic feet per minute should have automatic make-up air to prevent backdrafting. It doesn't just take one strong fan, though: if the range hood, dryer, and one or two bathroom fans are all running at the same time, it's not hard to put the house under negative pressure and create a backdraft.

Hydronic systems must be inspected regularly for leaks. The pipes always contain water, which cycles between hot and cold. This can put stress on the various joints and cause them to separate and leak.

Leaks in Hydronic Systems

Our first house had hydronic heat, with a boiler feeding a system of baseboard heaters throughout the house. As first-time homeowners, we didn't really know a lot about these systems, but got our education pretty quickly when one of the pipes going through the garage - the unheated garage - froze overnight and burst. And, of course, it was a Saturday evening, so any plumber was going to charge a premium for coming out to fix it.

Fortunately, Bob knew a bit about soldering, and had the necessary tools and supplies to repair the pipe. But it wasn't a quick or easy repair. The entire system had to be turned off and drained, the damage section cut out, and a new section put into place. Then the whole system had to be refilled, all the air purged, and only then could the boiler be turned back on.

This wasn't the last leak we had in the system either. Over the years, Bob dealt with several more, and each time we had to go through the same routine. And because every time we had a leak we had to refill the system with fresh water, the pipes ended up being exposed to more minerals and acids from the well water, which contributed to their deterioration.[45]

Leaks can also happen in radiators and convectors, and these are more difficult to repair. Baseboard convectors have to have the covers removed, the damaged pipes replaced, and the covers reinstalled, which just takes time. Radiators, however, are difficult to repair, and it is getting harder and harder to find companies that will restore them. New radiators are expensive, but used ones can sometimes be found at architectural salvage yards.

No Work/Access Area

It was the perfect attic access: the pull-down ladder was solid and moved smoothly and easily, and was installed according to the manufacturer's recommendations. I went up expecting to find an easy approach to the air handler that was installed in the attic.

---

45 *Well water is one of the major contributors to the deterioration of copper pipes. Any home on a well with acidic water and copper pipes needs to have a neutralizing system installed.*

This picture was taken from the attic access hatch. See any way to safely access the air handler? Me neither. Making this unit accessible is going to be difficult, and probably expensive.

Instead, I found a return air duct installed between the access opening and the walkway to the air handler, which I had to step over very carefully to avoid crushing. It didn't help that one of the truss webs was in the way, so I had to thread my way past these obstacles. Then there were more pieces of truss across the walkway to crawl under. Finally, I got to the air handler and discovered that there was no work surface in front of it; anyone servicing the unit would have to perch themselves on a single board laid across the joists and be very careful not to put a foot through the ceiling on either side.

Equipment installed in an attic space needs to be completely accessible for maintenance and repair, and there are specific requirements to meet. There must be a sturdy walkway with adequate headroom leading from the access opening all the way to the equipment. There must be a light fixture with a switch at the opening, and a receptacle to plug in any power tools. There also has to be a solid work surface that is at least the length of the equipment, and at least 24 inches deep. If one or more of these conditions is not met, it will end up in my report as a safety hazard.

HVAC equipment needs to be "readily accessible." This means getting to it can't require the use of portable ladders. Roof-mounted systems are fairly uncommon in residential applications, but every now and then we do run across them. If there is a system mounted on the roof, there needs to be a permanently installed ladder or staircase that gives access to the unit for maintenance or repair.

R-22 Coolant

About 20 years ago, scientists sounded an alarm: there is a hole in the protective ozone level over the Antarctic, and it's getting bigger. This is going to let in more dangerous radiation from solar rays. The cause of this expansion was the proliferation of chlorofluorocarbons, which were used as propellants in spray cans, and as refrigerants in air conditioning systems. The most popular and widest adopted was R-22, commonly known as Freon.

The problem comes when there are leaks in the air conditioning refrigerant tubes, and this happens a lot. The R-22 escapes and rises up through the atmosphere, contributing to ozone depletion.

In 1987, the Montreal Protocol established the timeline for the reduction and eventual elimination of R-22 as a coolant. The goal was a gradual decrease in both use and production, culminating in a complete ban by 2030.

The problem is that there are still a lot of R-22-filled air conditioning systems in use. If they're in good shape, there's no real issue, except that they are much less efficient than more current systems. Nowadays you cannot even buy a system that is designed for R-22 coolant; the standard is now R-410A.

This air conditioner is nearly twice its serviceable lifetime (about 14-15 years). It uses R-22 refrigerant, which is being phased out, which will make repairs more and more expensive as supplies dwindle.

If I see an air conditioner or heat pump that still uses R-22, I will advise my client that getting that system repaired is going to be increasingly expensive. As of this writing, the cost to refill an R-22 system is rapidly approaching the $1,000 mark. At the start of 2018, the manufacture of new R-22 has been halted, so only "recaptured" gas from old units is available. Eventually, even that will be prohibited.

Since the different coolants have different lubricants and different operating pressures, you can't simply flush out the old R-22 and replace it with R-410A. The only option is to completely replace the system.

As long as there are no leaks in the coolant system, and you know that the operating costs are going to be higher, you can certainly keep using an older system. My advice to my clients is to budget for a replacement, and to have the replacement done before the existing system breaks down.

Notes from the Field

"The boiler is well past its serviceable life and will need to be replaced."

This sentence may not seem like a big deal, but when we bought our home in 1997, it meant a big headache.

Old boilers are big, heavy, and may even be coated with a thick layer of asbestos-containing insulation. Removing them meant getting asbestos safely off of all the components first. The cost depends on how much material needs to be removed, but it can add up fast.

Next was getting the boilers out of the basement. The problem? They didn't fit through the door. How did they get them in then, you may ask. Simple: the foundation was dug, the slab poured, and the boilers placed in position. Then the rest of the house was built around them!

This is why we often see abandoned boilers left in place in older homes. Removing them was a significant expense: More than $6,000 (in 1997 dollars... more than $9,000 in 2018 dollars).

The old hydronic boiler on the left is coated with asbestos-containing insulation, and was abandoned in place and replaced with the "newer" one on the right. It was one of two old boilers in the house we bought in 1997. Both were removed during a renomation, but getting them out required cutting it into three pieces to get it through the door and up the stairs.

Inspection Tales

by Welmoed Sisson, Inspections by Bob

"*The laundry equipment appears to be at the end of its serviceable life.*"

©2018 Inspections by Bob, LLC

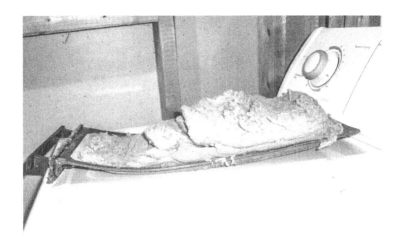

15
Laundry

Vinyl Dryer Vents

Clothes dryers are the cause of around one third of house fires in the United States. These fires usually happen due to lint built up in the vent, or even inside the dryer itself. Keeping the vent clear with regular maintenance is crucial, but equally important is the choice of venting material.

I typically see one of four types of dryer vent: rigid metal, smooth-wall flexible metal, metal foil coil, and vinyl coil. The best type to have is rigid metal; the worst is vinyl. The best ducts are also as short and straight as possible.

Dryer exhaust is hot and moist, and contains a lot of dust and lint. The moisture in the exhaust makes the lint sticky, and prone to collecting on the inside of the duct. Like a clogged artery, these lint buildups slow the airflow,

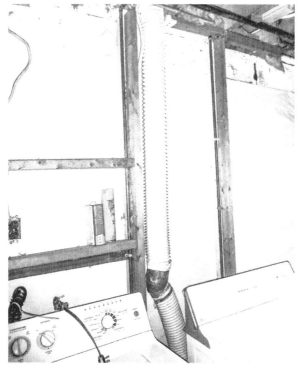

There are no dryer manufacturers who approve using this vinyl material for venting. It is important to read the installation instructions and follow all the recommendations for how to safely exhaust the pipe to the outside.

and attract more lint. Eventually the dryer cannot expel the exhaust, and works harder and harder; the heat builds up and can ignite the lint, and the result is a fire.

A lot of dryer vents are done incorrectly. There are actually two parts to a proper dryer vent. The first is the flexible piece called a vent connector. This is the piece between the dryer and the actual vent. It is supposed to be as short and straight as possible, with no kinks, bends, or other constrictions. It is designed to give you a little flexibility with the installation of the dryer, to accommodate different configurations in appliances.

The vent connector is attached to the actual dryer vent, which should be a smooth, rigid metal material. This part may not always be visible; it often runs inside the wall cavity. What you are not supposed to do is run the vent connector all the way to the exterior wall, and this is what we see so many times. There are no manufacturers who approve this kind of installation for their dryers, yet it is a common sight.

Dryer vents should be completely cleaned on a regular basis. In addition, the exterior outlet of the vent should be checked for any blockages; birds love to build nests in them.

Missing Catch Pan/Overflow Drain

Laundry areas were typically located in basements, away from living areas and out of sight. Eventually, architects caught on to the fact that most laundry was generated in the bedrooms, and towards the end of the 20th century started putting laundry rooms on the second floor. Convenient, yes, but when there's a water-using appliance over finished space, there's the risk of leaks and floods, and significant damage.

In basements, water from a burst washing machine supply hose can flow into a floor drain.[46] In an upstairs laundry room, that water would ruin flooring, damage framing, and destroy furnishings. So washing machines sit in plastic pans, which are connected to drain tubes leading to the exterior. If the home was designed with the laundry room on the second level, this drain was likely included. But if the laundry was originally in the basement,

Some builders have stopped installing overflow pans and external drains, claiming they aren't necessary, or that they don't know what size washer the client will put in. We recommend insisting on a tray and drain, especially if the laundry room is over living space.

---

46   *If there is a floor drain; many new houses are being built without general overflow drains in the basement.*

and the homeowner moves it to an upper floor, this drain may not be present, even if there is a pan under the washing machine.

One of the latest twists in washing machines is the introduction of front-loading machines on elevated platforms. These platforms often have drawers in them, and overflow pans block the drawers, so people remove the pans. This is not recommended!

These pans really aren't designed to contain a large flood (like from a burst hose). They are more for the smaller spill, like an overflow. If you see water in the pan, or see water flowing from the overflow tube outside, it's time to call for a repair.

Rubber Hoses

Water for the washing machine comes from two supply faucets, typically located on the wall behind and just above the washer. There should be shutoff valves here, and they need to be accessible so they can be shut off in the event of a leak. Unlike an outdoor hose bib, these faucets are not turned on and off for each use; the flow of water into the machine is controlled by valves within the washer itself.

This means the water in the hoses between the supply valves and the washer itself is always under pressure, so that it can flow immediately when

Washing machine supply hoses are under constant pressure; the valve inside the machine is what controls the flow. This means that if the rubber hose bursts, water will simply keep on rushing out until someone notices.

This dryer vent cover is completely packed with lint. These covers must be checked and cleaned on a regular basis; if the family does lots of laundry, this cover could fill up rapidly.

the washer is used. It also means that if there is a leak in the hose, the water will keep flowing until someone notices it and closes the shutoff valves. If the laundry is in the basement, a leak could go unnoticed until the next wash day, or starts affecting a more visible area. In a second floor laundry, such a leak can be disastrous, since it will quickly overwhelm the ability of any catch pan and drain tube to contain it.

I always recommend replacing any rubber washer hoses with braided stainless steel, as these are far less susceptible to the kind of blowouts that rubber hoses can have.

Clogged Vent Outlets

Many people get frustrated that birds or other animals will get into the various vent covers on the outside of the house and proceed to build a nest and raise a family. To thwart the unwelcome house guests, they will install screens or grates over the outlets. While this is fine for bath vents, it should not be done with dryer vents. The danger is that the screens will clog with lint, and that is a serious fire hazard.

Dryer vents should be cleaned at least once per year, all the way from the dryer to the outside. When I see a packed dryer vent cover during an inspection, it makes me wonder what other regular maintenance hasn't been done.

Inspection Tales

by Welmoed Sisson, Inspections by Bob

"Does the Chef convey?"

©2018 Inspections by Bob, LLC

16
Kitchen

Missing Anti-Tip

One of my favorite comments when reporting on a defect like this is that it's "a five minute job whose five minutes just hasn't come up yet." This simple little bracket prevents hundreds of injuries every year, but can't do its job if it is still waiting to be installed.

Anti-tip brackets have been required since 1991, and every manufacturer includes one with new free-standing stoves. These brackets are screwed to the wall or floor, and one of the rear legs of the stove slips into the bracket. This keeps the stove from - you guessed it - tipping forward.

There are lots of ways a stove could tip, even though you may think they are sitting firmly on the floor. For example, you open the stove to take

See how far the stove has tipped over? That's a sure sign of a missing or improperly installed anti-tip bracket. How do I get it to stay like that? My flashlight is propping it up from behind so I can step back quickly and take the picture.

the 20-pound turkey out for basting. Rather than lift it up to the cooktop (where you've probably got saucepans simmering), you set the pan on the open oven door. In doing this, you have changed the stove's center of gravity, and if that center moves forward enough, the stove will tip over, along with anything in and on it. This can seriously injure anyone in the way, by crushing or scalding. Another possibility is that a curious child will try to use the oven door as a stepstool to reach an upper cabinet.

It takes surprisingly little weight to make a stove tip forward. It's easy to test whether your stove has the proper bracket: try to tip it forward, either by pulling on the back or by pressing down on the open door.[47] If you can tip the stove forward more than an inch or so, either the bracket isn't there, or it wasn't installed properly.

Missing Wire Clamp on Grinder

Food waste grinders are a wonderful invention that help prevent clogged drains by chewing up large pieces of waste into a slurry. They

47 *Remember to take everything off the stove and out of the oven first; you don't want to hurt yourself!*

This under-sink food waste grinder is missing the clamp that protects the electrical conductors from damage. It's a surprisingly common defect, but one that is easy to overlook.

vibrate a lot, due to their powerful motors. Over time, this vibration can loosen the clamp holding the unit to the sink drain, which makes the vibration even worse. In addition to being an annoyance, this vibration can lead to a serious safety hazard.

The electrical wires supplying power to a grinder typically enter the unit on the bottom. This is out of sight for the most part. Then there's the typical under-sink storage jumble, where bottles and boxes are stuffed inside and shuffled around. It's not hard to see that the wire could be vulnerable to damage. To help protect the wire, there should be a clamp around it where it enters the body of the grinder. Without this clamp, the vibrations and the jostling could cause the wire to rub against the sharp metal edge of the grinder housing, cutting into the insulation and potentially exposing the bare wires inside. If this happens, there is a risk of arcing, which can lead to fire. It could also energize the entire grinder, along with anything metallic touching it, and deliver an electric shock to anyone coming into contact with it.

I always look at the bottom of the grinder when doing my kitchen inspections. It's a serious enough issue that I will remove items blocking my view[48].

Improper Dishwasher Installation

A dishwasher doesn't have a very powerful water pump to drain it; most are only around 15 psi, which is much less than the water pressure from your faucets. If it drains into a food waste grinder, which most of them do, and the sink drain gets clogged, it's not hard for that drain line to back up. This can lead to waste water flowing backwards into the dishwasher, and even back into the house's water supply pipes.[49]

There are two ways to keep this from happening. Either the dishwasher drain has an air gap device, or the drain line must form a "high loop". Some jurisdictions require air gap devices, due to the frequency of incorrect high loop installations.

So many times, I see the dishwasher drain line lying on the floor of the sink cabinet. It should be fastened securely up near the underside of the counter, as high as possible. Again, this is one of those five minute jobs whose five minutes just never came up. Some installers brush aside the concern by pointing out that the dishwasher "probably" has a high loop

Even a small clog in the dishwasher drain line can cause the air gap to act like a second faucet.

---

48   One of the few instances where I move a homeowner's belongings.
49   The technical term for this is a "cross connection" - any kind of situation where waste water can contaminate the drinking supply.

on the back of the unit. However, the loop must be readily visible, which means it needs to be inside the sink cabinet.

Rot/Growths Under Sink

If there are any kinds of rot or organic growths under a sink, there has been water leakage. Under a kitchen sink, this can come from a lot of different places. It can be the sink drain, or the dishwasher, or the supply pipes, or from a poorly-sealed undermount sink.

Sometimes the source is obvious: there's water visibly dripping from someplace. However, new leaks don't typically cause a lot of damage other than making a mess. The real problem comes with old, slow, persistent leaks. Many times people don't even know they have a leak because the cabinet under the sink is packed full of cleaning supplies. The problem only comes to light when the items are removed, and by then the damage can be significant. I have seen cabinets where the entire floor of the unit has rotted away.

Since these areas tend to be warm, moist, and dark, they are prime spot for organic growths. Once these have taken hold, the only solution is to remove all the affected materials and replace them. There's no amount of bleach that will completely remove organic growths once they've gotten into a porous surface.

Organic growths, duct tape repairs, rust and corrosion... not a pretty sight under a kitchen sink!

17
Bathroom

Loose Toilets

When I inspect a bathroom, one of the tests I perform is the "toilet wiggle." I lift the seat and stand astride the toilet, facing the tank, with the bowl between my knees. I then exert a gentle force from side to side to see whether the bowl is firmly attached to the floor. If it's not, I write it up. It seems like such a small thing; why do I make a fuss over it?

The connection between the toilet and the waste pipe isn't a permanent one; there's no glue, or weld, or even a clamp connecting the base of the toilet to the top of the waste pipe. It's really just gravity, plus a wax ring, and two bolts holding the toilet steady to the flange surrounding the pipe. So if that connection isn't absolutely solid, you can have leaks in the waste line. And those leaks are more than just water! One of the big problems with

Not what you want to see under a toilet! Stains like this are typically due to wobbly toilets and failed wax seals. Easy to see when it's over an unfinished area; over a living area, it will take a while for the stains to get through the drywall.

toilet leaks is that the damage is often hidden until it gets so serious you could face a collapsing floor.

Any wobbly toilet should not simply have the mounting bolts tightened. The entire toilet should be removed, and the floor and subfloor around the waste stack carefully examined to determine if there is any damage. The flange itself should also be checked for damage and replaced if needed. Once the necessary repairs have been made and the floor is stable, a new wax ring is installed, and the toilet re-seated and then bolted to the flange.

Toilets in full baths should also be sealed at the floor with caulk to prevent water from tubs or showers from penetrating around the soil pipe and causing problems. Caulking around toilets is a big area of disagreement among home inspectors and even among plumbers; some believe that caulking will prevent a homeowner from spotting a leak from under the toilet. However, virtually every toilet drain leak is preceded by a wobbly toilet, so if the toilet is secure, the drain is likely just fine.

Hot/Cold Reversed

Quick: which side of a faucet is the hot water control?

If you said "the left side," congratulations! That's correct. While this might not seem like such a big deal, it's actually a pretty important safety standard. Think of it this way: if there were no rule about which side was which, every sink and tub might have a different layout, and it would be a 50/50 chance that you'd turn the hot water on first and potentially burn yourself. Sure, the faucets might be marked, but what if your vision was impaired? With the standards in place, even a blind person could be confident in which they were turning on.

Here's a fun piece of trivia! The hot-on-left standard actually came about from the very early days of indoor plumbing. Kitchens often had pumps attached to the counter to provide water to the sink. Since most people were right-handed, the pumps were installed on the right. When pumps were replaced with water supply pipes, the tradition remained. So, when water heaters came around, it was natural that they would go on the left side.

Hot/cold reversal isn't necessarily a huge problem to fix; it's just a matter of disconnecting and reconnecting the proper feeders. But it can be a sign of sloppy plumbing work elsewhere in the house.

Gaps in Shower/Bath Walls

Water molecules are very, very tiny, and can fit through gaps and holes that are nearly invisible to the naked eye. If these gaps are in wet locations, like in shower walls or around bathtubs, these little molecules can add up to a huge headache.

It doesn't take a huge gap to cause enormous damage. Water seeps into cracks between tiles and is trapped inside the wall framing, where it causes rot. This is typically hidden, and is often only noticed when tiles start falling off, or stains appear on the ceiling below.

At one of our association's chapter meetings, we got a slide show from a bathroom remodeler who specialized in removing damaged shower and bath walls to repair the damage caused by water leaks. It was enough of an eye-opener to get us to go out the next day and fix the caulk and grout in our own bathrooms!

When we inspect bathrooms, we stand in the shower and/or tub and tap the walls, listening for the sound of loose tiles. We also look for areas of missing grout or caulk. Since we don't have that X-ray vision, we can't see behind the tiles to check for damage, but if the water has been getting behind there long enough, there will be damage. And to fix it, the tile and backer board will have to be removed. It's a big, messy, expensive job. A tube of caulk is so much cheaper!

Untempered Glass Doors

It's a fact of life that glass breaks. Regular glass will break into shards, with lots of sharp points and edges that can do severe damage if a person

A crack in the glass of a shower door is a clue that the glass is not tempered safety glass. Safety glass will never simply crack; instead, it will shatter into small pebbles that are less likely to cause injury.

contacts them, especially while falling. So why do showers often have glass doors?

Shower enclosures are made with a special type of glass called Tempered, or Safety Glass. It has been treated during the manufacturing process so that if broken, it will crumble into small chunks that are less likely to cause injury. This type of glass is usually identified by an etched label in one corner. If I don't see this label, I will write it up as potentially hazardous, since there is no other way to determine whether the glass is tempered.

Some jurisdictions allow tempered glass to be identified with stickers, which can wear off. Some areas don't require any kind of marking at all. In these cases, I recommend having documentation available to show that it is safety glass.

There are many rules about where safety glass should be used. Basically, any place where people might accidentally fall against a piece of glass, there should be safety glass. This includes windows along stairways, at lower landings, next to doors, and in doors themselves.

One of the places we see where safety glass is so often omitted is in new construction, where the design calls for a deck, but it will be added later. Any window that opens onto the deck is supposed to be safety glass, but since the deck isn't there during the original construction, the builder rarely installs the safety glass as it is more expensive. It's one of those little details that buyers of new construction usually forget to ask for.

Bath Exhaust Vent Problems

In older homes, only interior, windowless bathrooms had any kind of mechanical ventilation. Most of the time, the bathroom window was the only means of ventilation. But who wants to shower with an open window in sub-zero weather?

Most houses now have mechanical ventilation in every bathroom. These fans help remove humidity from showers and baths, as well as odors from toilets. Sometimes the only place we see vent fans are in toilet enclosures; if this is the case, we will recommend adding mechanical ventilation to the area with the bath and shower to prevent moisture damage.

What do you get when your bathroom exhaust vent pipe doesn't go all the way outside? You fill the attic with warm, moist air, which makes the roof framing a prime breeding ground for organic growths.

Bath fans should be vented directly to the exterior, either through the wall or the roof, and should have insulated ducting to prevent condensation. All too often, we see bath vents exhausting inside the attic, leading to organic growths on the framing and insulation. A common building practice used to be to extend the vent pipe through the attic and have the end a few inches away from the ridge vent. The result with this configuration is a section of roof sheathing with a lot of staining and evidence of water damage.

It's also a common defect to find bath fans installed without any ductwork at all; the fans simply exhaust into the attic right from the fan housing. In cases like this, there is typically a lot of damage to the insulation around the fan, along with signs of elevated moisture levels. I've seen attics that are so wet from improperly vented bath fans that the metal truss plates are dripping with moisture, and the insulation is completely saturated. And typically, the homeowner has no idea there is a problem; they paid to have fans installed and assumed the job had been done correctly.

One of the issues with older bath fans is that they are noisy. A bath fan should be quiet enough so that people will use it. Newer models are much quieter, and some even have the motor located closer to the vent termination than the bathroom itself.

Cracks don't have to be large to cause problems. They are an indicator of subfloor issues. It takes a lot of energy to crack a tile, especially if the crack extends across multiple tiles.

Bath fans can be on timers, or on motion sensors, to make them more effective and easier to use. The critical thing is that unless they are used, there is the potential for moisture to damage the surfaces in the bathroom, causing organic growths and odors.

Cracked Tiles

When I'm inspecting a bathroom, I pay attention to the floor as I am walking around. Does it feel secure? If the flooring is tile, I don't want to feel any movement or deflection at all. A spongy tile floor can lead to cracked tiles and grout. If I spot this, it can mean that the tile was laid over a subfloor that is too thin.

Cracked tiles aren't just a cosmetic flaw: they can let water penetrate the floor and damage the framing. Some cracks can also cause injury to bare feet; tile edges can be razor-sharp.

Fixing cracked tiles can depend upon what caused the damage. If there's a single spot of damage, it may be due to something being dropped onto the floor,[50] and can be repaired by replacing the affected tile. But

---

50   *I'll write this up as "mechanical damage."*

multiple cracks, or a line of cracking, or lots of cracks near the base of a toilet? These point to a more systemic problem that can mean the entire floor has to be taken up and properly replaced, with new subflooring and maybe even joist repair.

Accordion Drains

Drain pipes on kitchen and bathroom sinks is supposed to be smooth and "self-scouring" (that is, the water rushing through the drain pipe sweeps any debris out with it). Yet I constantly see flexible accordion pipes when I look at the drains!

Accordion pipe is often used when a fixture is updated and the new plumbing doesn't quite line up with the old. While this may save the homeowner a few bucks at the time, over the long run it can lead to chronic clogging and poor drainage. It is not meant for permanent use, and is meant only for emergency temporary repairs. This type of pipe traps debris in its folds and crevices, and this reduces the effective diameter of the pipe.

My recommendation for this type of drain pipe is always to replace it with smooth plastic, properly installed by a plumber. As I tell my clients, just because they sell it at the hardware store doesn't mean it's something you should be using!

Accordion drain pipes are meant for temporary repairs, not permanent use. They trap dirt and hair, are impossible to keep clean, and will clog much easier than a smooth pipe drain.

Notes from the Field

Another question I get a lot is "What's the worst house you've ever seen?"

That's actually a tough one to answer. All houses have issues, some more than others. With very few exceptions, houses can be brought back to life with enough time, energy, and especially money. I know it's possible because we've been there; we rescued a house in serious disrepair and restored it to good working order. Even so, it was an old house, so needed constant attention.

I think the one house that would qualify as "worst" would be an old farmhouse we inspected in upper Montgomery County. Plants threatened to swallow the front porch, which was rotted out. The cellar had active organic growth, and the water table was so high that a stream ran under the cellar slab (we could see it through a hole in the concrete). On the second floor, the beginnings of a renovation project were strewn all over, and there was a gap in the flooring where a wall once separated two rooms, and that gap went clear down to the bottom of the first level.

Did I mention they kept chickens in that room? Yep, and one of them had fallen into the gap at one time, and there was a hole bashed out of the first level wall that was created to rescue the chicken.

The gap that swallowed a chicken. Luckily only the cages were there during the inspection.

18
Garage

Non-Fire-Rated Door

Garages are meant to house vehicles, which contain gasoline, which is flammable. Gasoline vapors can be ignited by sparks, or a hot motor, or a hot surface, or lots of other ways. When something catches fire in a garage, it will put the entire house at risk unless the fire can be contained. One of the barriers is a fire-rated door between the house and the garage.

Doors from the garage to the living space are supposed to be rated for fire resistance; that means they are supposed to be able to withstand the spread of fire for at least 20 minutes. That's not a lot of time, but it's enough to let the occupants get out of the house. These rated doors have labels on the hinge side identifying them.

This mid-1970s house had a solid wood half-glass door (right) from the garage to the living space. It had a screen door as well, plus the attic above was contiguous with the rest of the house.

They should also be self-closing, typically with a special hinge. The door should not stay open on its own, but should swing shut and latch. This seals any fumes inside the garage and prevents them from getting into the house.[51] Sadly, the automatic closing mechanism is optional in some jurisdictions. And in new construction, once the final inspections are done and the Certificate of Occupancy issued, many homeowners replace the self-closing hinge with a regular hinge, since the self-closing door can be an annoyance when, say, bringing in groceries.

In some homes, I've even seen screen doors installed along with the solid door! Lots of times this is because they keep a pet in the garage, or they want to catch a breeze. My recommendation is always to remove the screen door and reinstall the self-closing mechanism. Without this protection, fumes or fire could spread rapidly into the house.

Garage Firewalls

Fire protection isn't limited to the door. Any surface that has living space on the other side must also resist the spread of fire. This includes the ceiling. However, many garages have secondary attics over them, with their own access hatches or stairs, and these access points are rarely fire-rated assemblies. This leaves these areas vulnerable to fire and fumes.

---

51   *Garage doors are also not allowed to open into sleeping areas, because of the risk of carbon monoxide fumes entering the house.*

Most of the time, these accesses are simple scuttles, with a piece of plywood or drywall set into a wooden frame, with wood trim holding it in place. In the event of fire, this type of assembly will fail very quickly, and if there are any breaks in the firewall between the attic garage and the house, fire will spread.

In some older single-level homes, it's not unusual to have a single attic that spans the entire house, including the garage, with pull-down stairs both in the living area and in the garage. Again, these stair assemblies are mostly made of wood, and are not rated for fire resistance. Having a continuous attic space increases the chances of fire spreading throughout the house.

Any access from the garage to the rest of the house should be fire-rated, with materials approved for the purpose (and labeled as such). Even small gaps in the firewall should be sealed up to prevent fumes from entering the house and to slow the spread of fire.

Any time there is living space on the other side of a garage wall, the wall must be rated to withstand a certain amount of fire damage. This is usually expressed in how much time it takes for fire to penetrate into the house. If there is living space above the garage, the ceiling needs to be included in the fireproofing plan. Sometimes I will see minor holes in the firewall, but every now and then I run across truly hazardous situations like this one. It should be no surprise that there were no visible permits for this addition, which included a garage with a family room over it.

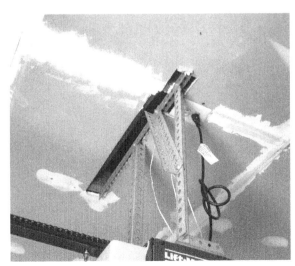

There really is no such thing as a "minor" hole in the fire separation wall between a garage and living space. Any gap can become a way for fumes or flames to spread into the house.

No Safety Wire

Garage doors are very heavy, and the only reason it is possible to open one by hand is because the weight of the door is counterbalanced by springs. When the door is closed, these springs stretch out, and when the door opens, the springs contract, carrying the majority of the weight of the door.

There are two common types of springs for garage doors; until recently, the most used were long springs stretching over the rails on both sides of the door. Nowadays, torsion springs are the preferred type; these are mounted horizontally above the door, and work by twisting rather than by stretching.

If you've ever twisted a paper clip back and forth, you know that eventually it's going to break instead of bend. This is because the movement has cause metal fatigue. The same thing can happen to a spring. Every time the garage door is opened or closed, there is a tiny bit of fatigue in the spring, and with enough fatigue, the spring will break. With the older side-mounted springs, this could make the entire assembly whip around with tremendous force, causing damage to anything near it and injury to anyone it hits.

There really is no way to prevent the fatigue and eventual breakage of the spring; the only thing is to keep it from doing damage when it does

This garage door spring is old, stretched out, and does not have a safety retaining wire running through it. There's no telling when it will break.

break. This is done with a safety cable threaded through the spring and anchored at both ends. Then if the spring breaks, the cable prevents it from flying around.

If I'm looking at an old garage door with springs that are stretched out and uneven, and I don't see a safety cable, I will think twice about testing the door. It's impossible to predict when a spring will break, and I won't want to be the one to open it that one time.

No Photoelectric Eyes

When I was a teenager, we moved to a house that had an attached garage with a great new feature: an automatic garage door opener. This was a lot of fun for us kids; it made leaving the house a game. We would press the button to start the door closing, then race to the front of the garage and duck out before the door closed all the way.[52]

Since 1993, garage door openers were required to have two safety reversing systems: first, the door should automatically reverse if it strikes a solid object (and this has been a requirement since 1982). Second, there should be a pair of photoelectric eyes mounted on the sides of the garage door opening, between four and six inches above the floor.

Yes, those are the photoelectric eyes that should be at the base of the garage door rails. We see this sort of defect more often than you may think.

---

52   *I think back about some of the stunts I pulled as a kid and see that it's a miracle I survived to adulthood.*

During a home inspection, I will test all the safety features present on the garage door opener. The approved method for testing the autoreverse is a solid object 1.5 inches thick. Since a regular piece of "two by four" lumber fits the bill, I have a piece of it in my tool kit, labeled "garage door tester." I hear about other inspectors using rolls of paper towels, or even their feet, to test doors. Neither of these is a standardized measuring tool!

If a door fails to autoreverse, it usually doesn't mean the whole thing needs to be replaced. Generally it just needs adjusting, which can be done in conjunction with a tune-up of the whole garage door assembly: lubricating the rails, checking the springs, and adjusting the opener.

This is the standard picture I take when a garage door fails to auto-reverse upon contact with a 1.5-inch solid object (a two-by-four). In my report, I typically caption this simply "Ouch."

Notes from the Field

Even Home Inspectors buy houses. Bob and I downsized in 2017, moving into a much smaller house suited for empty nesters.

The process was interesting. It was very, very hard to turn off our "home inspector" brain long enough to allow the "home buyer" brain to get a word in edgewise.

Our Realtor was so patient with us! She knew that showings would either be about a minute long, or three hours. While most buyers look first at kitchens, or bedrooms, or yards, we would go into a house and make a beeline for the basement.

Step one, look at the foundation. Any serious cracks or moisture? Okay, we're done. Next house!

Step two, check the electrical panel. Was it a bad brand (Check page 96 for the ones we call out)? Done! Next house!

If both those areas were okay, we would then start looking at the whole house in detail, including going into the attic and all those other hidden spaces. We would also have to remind ourselves to actually look at the rooms and spaces themselves, and try to envision ourselves and our stuff in those spaces too!

In the end, I think we looked at more than two dozen houses. Once we put in an offer on one, we hired our own home inspector to give the house yet another thorough going-over, just so that there would be no conflict of interest.

Proof that it's hard to turn off the Home Inspector brain. This picture of the dryer vent snaking through a bookcase was the only one I took during our first look at the house we eventually bought.

19
When to Call a Specialist

Septic Systems

A lot of home inspectors advertise that they perform "septic system tests." Most of the time, these are "dye tests." The inspector flushes a packet of dye down the toilet, then walks around the yard to see if there's any color bubbling up.

The problem with this kind of test is that it is pretty meaningless in terms of determining the health of a septic system. Proper septic tests involve locating and opening the cover of the septic tank, pumping it out, visually inspecting the interior to ensure the necessary elements are in place, and probing the leach field to check for biomat and other issues.

The big issue with septic systems is that when they fail, the repairs can be extremely expensive. Tanks themselves can last a long time, but the average life of a leach field might be as little as 15 to 20 years. After that, the field must be relocated. Some systems are built with two leach fields, with a valve that switches between the two fields every few years. This can greatly extend the life of a septic system, but most systems are only built with one field.[53]

Structural Engineer

A home inspector is a generalist. Most aren't structural engineers, although some are (and are usually more expensive). My training and experience have taught me to identify potential problems with the structural integrity of critical systems, but I am not an expert. If I think something might be a problem, but I'm not sure, I will recommend calling in a structural engineer for an evaluation.

An engineering consultation can take several forms. The simplest is where the engineer comes to the property and visually inspects the issue. They don't take complex measurements, but will observe the conditions and render an opinion on whether the issue is not a concern, or if it warrants further investigation. More involved engineering inspections include

The only proper way to test at septic system is to locate and open the lid, pump it out, and look inside. Don't trust so-called "dye tests" to give you an accurate picture of the health of the system

---

53   *After all, that extra field costs real money that builders don't want to "waste."*

extensive measurements and calculations, and may also require destructive testing (opening up finished surfaces) to get the complete picture of the problem. Engineers can also specify how repairs should be made.

Electrician

Taking the dead front off of an electrical panel is one of the most dangerous things home inspectors do, and one of the most important. On one inspection, I opened the panel and looked inside, and knew there were some connections that didn't look quite right.

The client wasn't keen on calling an electrician[54], so I sent a few pictures to one of the companies we had worked with before to get their opinion. Their response was along the lines of "Why hasn't that house burned down yet?" That got the client's attention, and they had this company come take a look. Turned out the problem was pretty darned serious: the electrician immediately decertified the panel, meaning it would require replacement, and called for extensive repairs to reduce the risk of an electrical fire.

There's a lot more to electricity than plugs and fixtures. Much of it is hidden behind walls, where a home inspector can't see it. There are a lot of defects we can identify, as shown in the Electrical System chapter, but in the real estate world, a generalist's opinion doesn't carry the weight of a trained

This house was a special case. The owners had started a renovation project to add on to the side of the house several years prior to this inspection, but never got further than excavating the foundation. Erosion has undercut the main house foundation and the chimney foundation, and there is no backfill to counteract the outward forces of the house. This one needed to be evaluated by a structual engineer as soon as possible to prevent a potential collapse.

---

54   *Yet another vendor wanting money during the home buying process.*

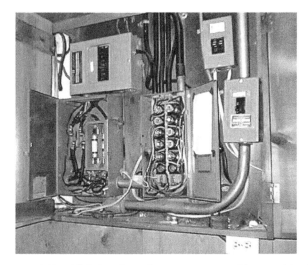

Cartridge fuses, screw-in fuses, circuit breakers, multiple subpanels, nirtually no labeling, and about 400 Amps demand on 125 Amp service. It's a miracle the house hand't burned down.

specialist. This is why, when we spot problems with the system, we will recommend bringing in an electrician to take a closer look at the problem.

Sometimes we do this out of an abundance of caution since some issues can be serious fire hazards (aluminum wiring, worn service cables), and some are life safety issues (lack of GFCIs, no safe panel access). If there is a danger to people or property, the defect needs to be fixed.

Other times we call for an electrician when we find electrical equipment that is outdated, or when we find certain brands of panels. In these cases, the electrician may come in and look at the problem and declare that it's fine, and say the home inspector is just being paranoid. My response is always to tell my client to have the electrician put their opinion in writing, on official letterhead, with their license number. That way, if there is a problem in the future, the electrician will bear the liability for declaring it safe.

Chimney Sweep

Fireplaces are precise systems that have a very important job: contain a dangerous fire and safely exhaust its combustion products out of the home. If one or more of the components aren't working properly, the result could be catastrophic.

There are so many ways a fireplace or chimney can fail: gaps in the firebox, broken damper, cracks in the flue, creosote build-up, detachment from the house, or even just poor design and construction. Any one of these issues could lead to a costly repair bill.

Chimney repairs are almost always expensive. The problem isn't that the repairs are hard to do; it has more to do with getting to the areas that need to be fixed. You may think that some missing mortar on the outside of the chimney is pretty minor, but it may mean that the chimney must be demolished down to where the problems are, and then rebuilt. This is because exterior symptoms can mean problems with the interior, and since the risk of fire is high, chimney companies tend to be very careful about making sure they fix things properly.

In the chapter on fireplaces and chimneys, I wrote about some of the issues we see during our home inspections, and that there are a lot of items we cannot see. If you are buying a home that has a masonry fireplace (that is, a traditional wood-burning fireplace with a brick firebox and chimney), we always recommend getting a Level II inspection to get an expert's opinion on the condition. This way, if the system ends up needing expensive repairs, you will know about it before closing, and can take it into account when negotiating with the seller.

This chimney needed to have the top 15 courses removed and replaced due to cracking and spalling. Work like this requires scaffolding, as the projecting chimney should never be used to support a ladder.

Inspection Tales
by Welmoed Sisson, Inspections by Bob

20
Environmental Hazards

Critters, Dead or Alive

Building a house interrupts nature. The animals that lived where a house now stands still have to live somewhere; many of them have discovered that there are comfortable places inside a house where they are normally not disturbed: attics, crawl spaces, or inside walls.

Bob did an attic inspection a few years ago that started out pretty normally. It was an older home, with structural masonry construction on the outside walls. As is our normal practice, he lifted up the scuttle cover and poked his head in to get a quick look at the attic.[55]

Immediately, he heard an odd chittering sound. He looked up at the gable and saw a colony of bats hanging from the peak of the wall, looking

---

55   *My first look tells me whether I can safely enter the attic: is there a safe walking surface? Is it too hot? Are there live critters?*

Nesting material in the attic can harbor all sorts of nasty pathogens. Don't enter a space like this without a respirator and gloves. Better yet, call a specialist to deal with it.

at him. Now, neither of us is typically rattled by critters, but bats can carry rabies, so he quickly closed the attic scuttle and wrote in his report that the bat colony had to be removed by a qualified wildlife removal company.[56]

Once the bats are removed (usually by installing what's called an Exclusion Device), the attic has to be cleaned to remove any traces of feces and urine, as these can also harbor pathogens. Cleaning may involve removal of contaminated insulation, soaked drywall, and/or removal of framing. If framing has to be cut out and replaced, a structural engineer may be needed to specify how to do the repair so the integrity of the roof isn't compromised.

Other live critters we've seen in attics include snakes, mice, squirrels, birds, wasps, bees, and raccoons. We've also seen our share of droppings, nesting materials, snake skins, and carcasses. All of these will create hazardous wastes that will need to be professionally remediated.

Lead Paint

A house built prior to 1978, when the sale of lead paint was banned, is presumed to have lead paint unless proved otherwise. What a lot of people don't realize is that even houses built after the ban went into effect could also have surfaces covered with lead paint. That's because while the sale of lead paint was prohibited, the use of it was not.

56   *You should never kill bats; they are incredibly important for insect control.*

Lead paint was prized for its lustre, durability, and color retention. It was most often used on surfaces that would be subjected to wear, such as window frames, exteriors, and doors. When the ban was announced, painting companies started buying up as much lead paint as they could, so it's not unusual to see houses built in the 1980s or even later to have it.[57]

The dangers of lead poisoning have been well documented: it has a devastating effect on children, leading to mental disabilities and multiple health issues. Lead paint was a prime source, but contrary to common beliefs, it's not because children eat paint chips. Lead paint is very bitter, so most children won't knowingly put chips in their mouths more than once. The real issue is dust.

Every time a surface covered with lead paint is disturbed, either by brushing against it, or by sliding open a window or opening a door, a tiny amount of paint particles is released into the air. These particles settle on the window sills, floors, and other flat surfaces. Children then come into contact with these surfaces and the particles get onto their hands, and when their hands go into their mouths, the particles are ingested.

Sometimes lead paint is covered up with regular latex paint over the years. If this is done on areas that don't get disturbed at all, this is typically an acceptable solution. But for areas that will be subject to any kind of

It's possible to test for exposed lead paint with these LeadCheck™ chemical swabs. If the tested surface turns pink, there is lead in it. To detect concealed lead, an X-ray inferometer test is needed.

---

57   *A fellow inspector told me he had found lead paint throughout a house built in 1996!*

abrasion, like windows, the lead paint should be stripped off and the surface repainted.

Regulations require any contractor doing work on a pre-1978 property to perform a lead paint test if they suspect its presence.[58] This isn't just a quick surface swab test, but rather a very specific sampling protocol must be followed and the samples sent to a certified lab for testing. Or, a certified lead tester can use a very sophisticated tool called an XRF Analyzer, which can detect lead paint even if it is covered up by repainting or wallpaper.

If lead paint is found, any work performed must be done by EPA-certified lead-safe contractors, and the work must be scrupulously documented. Fines for undocumented work can be steep: over $35,000 per occurrence.[59]

Asbestos

This mineral has been used for thousands of years, first for making cooking pots more durable. Its use really expanded in the 19th century,

Asbestos was commonly used in pipe insulation, especially for steam or hydronic heating systems. Removal should only be done by a qualified remediation company due to the risk of contaminating the rest of the house.

---

58   *Just because a house is built before 1978 doesn't mean it will have lead paint. The stuff was expensive, so only higher-end homes had it.*
59   *If six windows are scraped and repainted without following the protocols, each window is an occurance, so the fine could be over $200,000.*

Sometimes it's easy to make a definitive statement about whether insulation could have asbestos: These bags are branded "ZONOLITE," which was mined in Libby, MT.

when the first asbestos insulation came on the market. It was popular because of its natural fire-resistant properties and was widely used for insulation on pipes, in flooring, and for exterior siding and shingles.

In the 1930s, doctors became aware of health problems in people who worked in asbestos mines, and started diagnosing workers with asbestosis[60]. Asbestos workers could also develop mesothelioma, a form of lung cancer. Both these diseases take a long time to develop; it could be a decade or more after asbestos exposure for symptoms to appear. The big problem is that it's not known how much - or how little - exposure leads to either of these diseases, and there is still a lot of asbestos present in houses.

During an inspection of an older home, I will be looking for evidence of asbestos-containing materials. Some of the more common ones are:

- Floor tiles measuring 9 inches by 9 inches
- Pipes covered in material that resembles white corrugated cardboard
- In-floor ductwork lined with Transite
- Vermiculite attic insulation

Asbestos removal must be done by trained professionals. If it is not removed using strict environmental controls, there is a huge risk of releasing asbestos fibers into the air, where they could be distributed

---

60   Literally, "asbestos disease."

These tiles have the hallmark size and the mottled dark streaks that were typical of asbestos-containing tiles. The mastic often had more asbestos fibers in it than the tiles did.

throughout the house via the ductwork. And since there is no known safe level of exposure for asbestos, this kind of contamination can mean extremely expensive remediation: every single surface that could have been exposed to the fibers (ducts, floors, walls, furniture, clothing, carpeting, stuffed animals, etc.) must be decontaminated or discarded.

As mentioned before,[61] one of the common items we find are the 9 x 9 floor tiles. They're typically in the basement. With these tiles, the recommended remediation method is to cover them with a solid flooring, such as a good sheet vinyl. This method is called encapsulation, and is an effective method of ensuring that no fibers will be released in the future.

Radon

Radon is a byproduct of the decay of uranium. It occurs naturally in the soil, especially in areas with a lot of granite. It's the second leading cause of lung cancer, causing an estimated 21,000 deaths per year.

Even before it was identified as an element, people recognized its hazardous effects. In ancient times, miners developed what was called a "wasting disease" due to their exposure underground. It was isolated in 1899, but wasn't linked to lung cancer until the 1950s. People didn't really

---

61   *See Chapter 11, Interior Elements.*

become aware of it as a household problem until 1984, when an employee at a nuclear power plant set off radiation detectors prior to entering the facility. The contamination was eventually traced to his home, which was tested and found to have a radon level of 2,700 picocuries per liter (pCi/L).[62]

The Environmental Protection Agency (EPA) established an "actionable level" for radon of 4 picocuries per liter (pCi/L). While this is still not a "safe" level, it was chosen as a compromise between risk and cost. The World Health Organization (WHO) has recommended that any home with levels higher than 2.7 pCi/L should have a remediation system installed to bring indoor radon down to 0.4 pCi/L, which is equivalent to typical outdoor levels.

Why is Radon so dangerous? The primary reason is that it is the only gaseous form of the uranium decay process. It has a half-life of just a few days, but if it is inhaled, it will continue to decay inside the lungs, producing radioactive particles that will damage lung tissue. It is a fairly dense gas,

Radon abatement system fans should not be located within the envelope of the house. This fan is under the stairs to the partially-finished basement. It needs to be relocated either to the attic, or to an outside pipe that terminates above the roofline.

---

62   *The cancer risk factor equivalent to smoking several hundred packs of cigarettes every single day.*

The organic growths in this 1900 farmhouse were in full bloom in the very damp cellar. We insisted our client wear a respirator when he went in there.

which is why tests are performed in the lowest habitable levels of a home, and why those ancient miners were affected so badly.

Any home that tests high for radon should have a remediation system installed. This is simply a pipe that extends through the basement slab into the gravel, extending up either through the house or on the exterior, terminating above the roof. A fan is installed along the pipe, which runs constantly and draws the air (and the radon) up and out before it can seep into the house. A properly-installed system will reduce even high radon levels down to background levels; even that nuclear plant worker's home was successfully remediated.

Organic Growths and "Wood Destroying Organisms"

Houses exist in a natural environment. They're not sterile, antiseptic or hermetically sealed. People come and go, and with them come unintended passengers: insects, mold spores, bacteria. It's just a fact of life.

Most of the time, in a well-ventilated and well-maintained house, these things do not thrive. They dry out, go dormant, or die, and end up as part of normal house dust. But if the environmental conditions are right, they grow and flourish, and can cause a lot of problems for the people in the house, as well as for the house itself.

A common question for home inspectors is whether they do mold testing. If I tested houses for mold, I would almost certainly find evidence of it in just about every house. It's a normal component of our environment, and unless you live in a sterile bubble in a hospital, it's all around you too. The important issue is whether it is growing.

Mold spores need moisture to grow. Take away the moisture, and the spores go dormant.[63] If the water comes back, the spores will grow again.

Spores also need a food source. Your house has a lot of it: framing, furniture, food spills on carpets... anything organic can support mold growth. This is why we point out the hazards of hidden damage to framing when we see gaps in exterior finishes. Water gets in, the spores wake up, and they start feeding on the framing.

Our "mold tester" is our nose. If there's a musty, moldy smell in the house, or in an area of the house, there is almost certainly an organic growth nearby. The task is figuring out where it's growing, and how to dry that area out and keep it dry so it stops. A formal "mold test" will identify the species of mold that is growing, but honestly, that information isn't terribly useful unless you have a specific allergy to one type of mold.

If someone in the household has a severe respiratory illness, or is immune-compromised, getting an indoor air quality expert's help may be helpful. The very best type of expert is an Industrial Hygienist, but they usually don't do residential work.

The termite inspector was on site while I was there, and identified these as swarming termintes. The basement was riddled with tubes.

---

63   Dormant, not dead. Killing spores is a lot more involved.

Other wood-destroying organisms[64] exist naturally in the soil and try to make their way into your house because they are attracted to the smell of decaying wood. Colony members go exploring to find new food sources, and if they find some tasty soft wood that has gotten damp, they send word to their friends and the horde descends. If you've ever seen lines of tube-like mud creeping from the dirt up the side of the house and underneath the siding, those are likely termite tubes.[65] These tubes can show up outside or inside, and if you see them, you should be calling a professional pest control company because the hidden damage could be substantial.

I once inspected a large, $2 million property that had been sitting vacant for nearly a year. The termite inspector happened to be there at the same time, and pointed out a windowsill covered with dead and dying insects. "That's a termite swarm," he told me. The window frame and trim was riddled with termites. The more we looked, the more infested wood we found: in other windows, even in some interior walls. We finally found the tubes in the far end of the basement! I wrote in my report that the entire basement would likely have to be gutted to reveal the extent of the

This old firebomb was hanging over the furnace, still intact, still with its heat-sensitive trigger in place, and still full of hazardous and potentially toxic chemicals.

---

64   *I can't say "termites" because I'm not a trained pest control expert.*
65   *Termites are dark-loving creatures; they make the tubes to hide from the sun and to keep themselves from drying out.*

damage. Typically, termite remediation involves removing all the affected materials (framing, drywall, insulation, etc.) until there is zero evidence, then removing about a foot more just to be sure. In extreme cases, the entire house may have to be "tented" - essentially, wrapping the house in plastic and fumigating it with pesticides.

Some home inspectors also do termite inspections, but we recommend calling a separate company to perform these. Because the potential for damage is so great, you want to get someone who specializes in this kind of work, and has had a lot of training and continuing education in this one topic, rather than someone who offers it as an add-on because they once took a two-day training seminar.

Pest control companies typically can also issue a warranty certificate. The certificate is renewed every year by getting an annual inspection. If you have such a warranty and still end up with termite damage, the issuing company will cover some or all of the repairs.

Hazardous or Explosive Materials

Home Inspectors often run across all manner of really dangerous stuff, including firearms, explosives, or chemicals. My general rule when encountering something like this is to recommend having the item removed by a certified Hazardous Waste removal company. In some cases I might even suggest contacting the local fire department for their input on how to safely dispose of something.

Case in point: every so often I will see an old device called a Fire Bomb. These were rudimentary safety devices intended to put out a fire in a furnace or boiler. The chemical in these glass globes was typically Carbon Tetrachloride (CTC). Exposure to CTC can cause a host of physical problems to the respiratory, kidney, thyroid, brain and reproductive systems; some of these effects can be fatal. What's worse is that when CTC is exposed to the heat, it can produce phosgene gas, which was used as a chemical weapon in World War I. Not really something to have hanging around the house in a fragile glass container!

When we encounter these devices during an inspection, we inform everyone present that this is a hazardous item that should not be touched, and must be safely disposed of by a qualified hazardous materials company..

21
Conclusions

Buying a house is a stressful time. There are a million details to think about, and everyone seems to want to sell you something. It's important to remember to slow down and take a step back from everything once in a while. It's so easy to get caught up in the excitement of finding your new home and it's so easy to fall in love with a place without knowing exactly what you are in for.

A home inspector's job is to take the bloom off the rose. You want us to identify all the issues that could affect the safety of the people living in the home, and all the issues that could mean significant expenses for repairs or upgrades, either now or in the near future. We aren't there to scare you, or to discourage you from buying the house,[66] but do want you to

---

[66]   Except one time we did; the basement was coated with organic growths and the buyer's wife was severely asthmatic; we suggested that they rethink the purchase. They did.

know as much as possible so you can go into the purchase process with the information you need to make an informed decision.

This book may have you feeling like every house is a death trap. True, we've seen houses that were in terrible shape, but even those can be saved, with enough money. Sometimes lots of money. I just feel bad for buyers who think they've got a gem, only to find out the house needs major repairs and upgrades, and they haven't got the budget for anything but new paint.

The harsh truth is that no house will last forever. Unlike the ancient houses that were built with stone, houses built with organic materials will eventually deteriorate, rot, and fail. Very few houses in the United States were built before 1800, and even those have been heavily modified and updated. With proper construction methods, regular maintenance, and taking care of small problems before they have a chance to become big ones, you stand a better chance of ensuring your home will last as long as possible.

Some problems with houses are directly the result of either poor material choices or poor construction practices. Those really can't be prevented when dealing with existing houses; even in new construction, builders won't always fix something we call out unless it's an obvious error. The rest of a house's issues can be attributed to deferred maintenance, or just a lack of attention. People simply don't see the little incremental changes in their homes. They get used to them, and that makes it easy to let some things slide.

The best way to ensure a house lasts and is safe to live in is to get regular inspections. This will catch the little things while they're still little, and help you plan and budget for the big things that will need doing in the coming years.

Thanks for reading!

Share your own stories of home ownership at
101ThingsYouDontWant.com

Keep in touch and find out about future publications on FaceBook!
facebook.com/NinovanBooks

Acknowledgements

This book has been the culmination of two years of thinking, planning, dithering, scribbling, worrying, researching, procrastinating, and, ultimately, simply writing it all down. So many people have cheered me on in the process, offering suggestions and ideas, reading drafts, and gently but firmly kicking my rear into gear when I felt discouraged.

Helena B. took one of the first looks at my rough concept and encouraged me to dive into the adventure of actually creating a book in the first place.

The O.G. Group cheered me on, even as I had so many doubts about whether it could all be done, or if I was fooling myself into thinking that anyone would even be interested in reading a book like this.

Elizabeth F. held onto the check that was my motivation to get it all wrapped up (now shred it, please!).

Various inspectors both in person and online, who gave me valuable feedback when I wasn't quite certain if what I was writing was the most accurate.

The American Society of Home Inspectors, and the members of my local chapter, MAC-ASHI, for never making assumptions about my abilities and welcoming me into the profession from the very beginning.

The Workforce Development Department at Frederick Community College, for giving me the opportunity to teach the home inspection certification class. Having to present all this material to students has kept me on my toes about the finer details of the systems and standards we have to know.

My wonderful kids, who took time out from their own busy lives to help with some of the polishing of the book: Ian helped with editing, and Diana helped make the pictures look their best.

And, of course, to my wonderful husband Bob, who started Inspections by Bob in 2003 with an enormous leap of faith, and who then waited patiently until I realized it would be a great idea to join him. Working together has been a joy, and a challenge at times too, and I wouldn't want it any other way. My love, I'm so happy to be your business partner and to have you as my best friend, too.

Appendix

I: Helpful Websites

Inspections by Bob   inspectionsbybob.com
     We have a lot of articles and blog posts on our site, along with our "Hall of Shame," with lots more pictures of defects we have found during our 15 years of home inspections.

American Society of Home Inspectors   ashi.org
     Find an inspector in your area

Consumer Product Safety Commission   cpsc.org
     Information on recalls for appliances and more

Zillow   zillow.com
     Good resource for locating information on homes (especially sales history)

Consumer Reports   consumerreports.org
     Good for finding reviews and ratings for appliances

Building Intelligence Center   buildingcenter.org
     Comprehensive online database of HVAC and water heater serial numbers to determine their age

Mr. Fix-It   misterfix-it.com
     Articles on home repair and maintenance from Tom Feiza, author of "How to Operate Your Home," which we give to clients at each inspection

Inspectapedia   inspectapedia.com
     The Free Online Encyclopedia of Building & Environmental Inspection. Everything you ever wanted to know about houses and what goes into them.

II: Recommended Maintenance

Spring

- ☐ Check window screens for damage
- ☐ Test all windows for proper operation and repair any that do not open and close easily
- ☐ Clean and inspect deck and replace corroded components
- ☐ Check roof for any damage from snow or storms
- ☐ Test the sump pump for proper operation
- ☐ Clean and inspect gutters and downspouts
- ☐ Have the air conditioning system serviced
- ☐ Inspect the exterior and repair any damage
- ☐ Change furnace duct dampers from "Winter" to "Summer"
- ☐ Have lawn mowing equipment serviced
- ☐ Have driveway and walkways repaired as needed from winter damage

Summer

- ☐ Trim branches and shrubs from around the air conditioner condensor (18"-24" inches)
- ☐ Check trees on property for signs of poor health

Autumn

- ☐ Have the furnace or boiler serviced
- ☐ Check the attic to make sure insulation is in good condition
- ☐ Remove hoses from outdoor faucets and turn off water supply to all exterior hose bibs
- ☐ Trim bushes and trees to provide 6-12 inches of clear space from the house exterior and any utility wires
- ☐ Have the chimney inspected and cleaned
- ☐ Check for drafts around doors and windows and seal with caulk, foam, or weatherstripping
- ☐ Have any snow removal equipment serviced

Winter

- ☐ Inspect foundation walls in basements and crawl spaces for leaks after storms
- ☐ Monitor the roof for icicles and ice dams

Monthly

- ☐ Change HVAC filter
- ☐ Test GFCI and AFCI breakers and receptacles; have any faulty ones replaced
- ☐ Replace or clean range hood filters

Annually
(not seasonally dependent)

- ☐ Have garage doors and openers inspected and serviced
- ☐ Flush the water heater to remove sediment
- ☐ Clean dryer vents and check that vent covers are working properly

Every Few Years

- ☐ Test well water quality
- ☐ Test radon level
- ☐ Replace backflow valve on fire supporession sprinkler system
- ☐ Have roof inspected and any necessary repairs performed

Every 7-10 Years

- ☐ Replace all smoke alarms
- ☐ Have a Home Checkup home inspection performed

III: Chapter Heading Captions

Page 3	*This was a quick promo shot for an article I was interviewed for. Too bad they didn't use it.*
Page 7	*My client took this shot of me while I was deep into the crawl space, trying to find the main water shutoff valve. Turns out there wasn't one.*
Page 11	*I love coming across random historical stuff in attics. I do my best not to disturb anything I find; these were laying just like this on the floor. I clearly remember each of these occasions.*
Page 15	*Even though it hadn't rained in several days, the grounds surrounding this particular property were extremely soft and mushy. This was highlighted by the tire tracks of the truck that had tried to remove the dumpster in the yard.*
Page 27	*The "man door" -- the exit from the garage directly outside -- is in an awkward location here. Watch that first step.*
Page 35	*I spotted this while walking around the inner harbor area in Baltimore, MD. There were actually quite a few of these decks perched on top of roofs. I wonder if they were built with permits?*
Page 41	*This house had one of the worst exteriors we had seen (and the interior was pretty bad too). Moss and rot everywhere.*
Page 49	*This was the pier under a kitchen in an old 1800s farmhouse. We called it the "Jenga Pier" and walked very carefully in the room above it.*
Page 57	*Truss chord cut to install an air handler. One of the rules of truss construction is that no field modifications are allowed without documentation. Cutting a truss web weakens that part of the roof.*
Page 65	*This door scraped along the ceiling due to serious sagging. It should be no surprise that this was in the same house as the Jenga Pier on page 49.*
Page 71	*When you add on a second level, it's a good idea to extend the chimney while you're at it. Chimneys should be at least two feet above anything within ten feet.*
Page 81	*It's nice to want to use attic spaces, but the minimal head clearance and short guard rails made this one a hazard.*
Page 93	*Who needs a plug? Just stick the wires into the receptacle and you're in business. Yes, this was live.*
Page 111	*Did they think the water was going to flow uphill into this drain?*
Page 123	*This beast is a gravity furnace. They're called "Octopus Furnaces" for obvious reasons. They have no fans or pumps; no moving parts means they tend to last a long, long time. However, they are horribly inefficient.*
Page 135	*Please remember to clean your filter before putting a load in the dryer.*

Page 141   The liner in this refrigerator door is cracked clear through. This can't be fixed; either the whole door should be replaced, or simply replace the entire fridge. I moved an item to take this picture; The rest of the fridge was pretty empty. Maybe the seller was trying to conceal a defect?

Page 147   In this "time capsule" mid-century modern house, the master bath was entirely pink. This included all the fixtures, the cabinet, the counter, the walls, and even the ceiling.

Page 157   If we can't see it, we can't report on it. We advise our clients to be extra careful checking the area on the final walkthrough to make sure the stuff wasn't hiding some surprises.

Page 165   This is the Rocky Springs Church Schoolhouse, which was across the street from a house we were inspecting. It is currently undergoing restoration.

Page 171   Although it's not technically part of a home inspection, I will warn people if I see a large wasp nest such as this one. You never know if your client, their agent, or anyone else visiting the property could have a life-threatening allergy to insect stings.

Page 183   I taught a class at InspectionWorld 2015 in Philadelphia on inspecting kitchen appliances. It was my first taste of teaching home inspection, and I loved it.

Page 185   At InspectionWorld 2018, I had the honor of meeting Ron Passaro, who holds ASHI member number 1. My ASHI number is 252093.

Colophon

Headlines: Franklin Gothic Bold

Body: Garamond

Cover Design: Welmoed Sisson

Created in Adobe InDesign

All photographs by Bob Sisson or Welmoed Sisson

(photograph on page 189 by Universal Photo)

Author Photograph by
Jessica Patterson Photography

About the Author

Welmoed Sisson is an ASHI-Certified Inspector in Frederick, Maryland. She and her husband Bob own and operate Inspections by Bob, providing residential home inspections in the central Maryland area.

Sisson is President of the MAC-ASHI chapter of the American Society of Home Inspectors (ASHI), and also serves as Chair of the Public Relations Committee for ASHI. She has taught seminars at the annual ASHI conference, InspectionWorld, as well as at other ASHI chapters.

In 2016, she joined the staff of Frederick Community College as an Adjunct Professor, and teaches the Home Inspection Pre-Licensure class there.

Made in the USA
Middletown, DE
24 April 2020